THE OUTBREAK OF
THE CIVIL WAR

MILESTONES
IN
AMERICAN HISTORY

THE OUTBREAK OF THE CIVIL WAR

A NATION TEARS APART

HEATHER LEHR WAGNER

CHELSEA HOUSE
PUBLISHERS
An imprint of Infobase Publishing

Chelsea House
An imprint of Infobase Publishing
132 West 31st Street
New York NY 10001

Library of Congress Cataloging-in-Publication Data
Wagner, Heather Lehr.
    The outbreak of the Civil War : a nation tears apart / Heather Lehr Wagner.
        p. cm.—(Milestones in American history)
    Includes bibliographical references and index.
    ISBN 978-1-60413-053-9 (hardcover)
    1. United States—History—Civil War, 1861–1865—Causes—Juvenile literature.
    2. United States—History—Civil War, 1861–1865—Juvenile literature.   3. United
    States—Politics and government—1849–1861—Juvenile literature.   4. Slavery—United
    States—History—Juvenile literature.   5. Secession—Southern States—Juvenile
    literature.   6. Davis, Jefferson, 1808–1889—Juvenile literature.   7. Lincoln, Abraham,
    1809–1865—Juvenile literature.   I. Title.   II. Series.

    E468.9.W25 2009
    973.7'11—dc22   2008024153

Chelsea House books are available at special discounts when purchased in bulk quantities
for businesses, associations, institutions, or sales promotions. Please call our Special Sales
Department in New York at (212) 967–8800 or (800) 322–8755.

You can find Chelsea House on the World Wide Web at http://www.chelseahouse.com

Series design by Erik Lindstrom
Cover design by Ben Peterson

Printed in the United States of America

Bang NMSG 10 9 8 7 6 5 4 3 2 1

This book is printed on acid-free paper.

All links and Web addresses were checked and verified to be correct at the time of
publication. Because of the dynamic nature of the Web, some addresses and links may
have changed since publication and may no longer be valid.

CONTENTS

President of the Confederate States

It was February 1861, and Jefferson Davis and his wife, Varina, were in the garden of their Mississippi plantation trimming a rose bush. The plantation, which Davis called Brierfield, stretched across 800 acres (about 325 hectares) in Davis Bend, 20 miles south of Vicksburg. Davis's older brother Joseph had a large plantation next to Davis's property.

Davis's plantation had slaves providing labor, but on that February day it was Jefferson Davis himself who was pruning the roses. There would not be many more peaceful days to spend on simple chores. War between the states was coming, Davis was certain, and he had an important role to play. He had spoken to the governor of Mississippi a few weeks earlier and was promised the job he wanted. The 53-year-old Davis had known success in battle, and had proven to be courageous and heroic. So, when war came, Davis would serve as major general in the Mississippi militia.

Davis was born in what was then called Christian County, Kentucky, on June 3, 1808. (There is some confusion about the year of Davis's birth, however, with Davis himself occasionally stating it as 1807. He confessed that he was never sure, and family records were lacking on this point.) He was the youngest child of Jane Cook Davis and Samuel Emory Davis, a Revolutionary War veteran. Most of the Davis sons were given Biblical names—names such as Joseph, Samuel, Benjamin, and Isaac. But when it came to his youngest son, Samuel Davis chose to name him Jefferson F. Davis after the current president, a man he greatly admired: Thomas Jefferson. Many historians, including Hudson Strode and Shelby Foote, suggest that the *F* stood for *Finis*—meaning "end" or "conclusion." According to historians, Samuel Davis gave his tenth child this name in the belief that Jefferson F. would be the last child, which he was.[1]

Many men of Jefferson Davis's age would claim their allegiance and their fiercest loyalty not to the United States, but rather to their home state. Davis moved often during his youth and early adulthood, though, so he did not possess this kind of state loyalty. He lived in many states, chiefly in the southern United States, so it was to the South as a whole that he felt the strongest ties.

Davis's family moved to Louisiana shortly after his birth, and soon thereafter continued on to Mississippi. They settled in Woodville, southeast of Natchez and 40 miles from the Mississippi River, where Samuel Davis soon built a prosperous cotton farm. Jefferson Davis attended several schools, first within walking distance of his home, and then, when he was about eight years old, the St. Thomas College boarding school near Springfield, Kentucky. After two years, his mother missed her youngest child, and Jefferson was allowed to go home and return to the small log schoolhouse where he had begun his education.

Jefferson Davis was the first and only president of the Confederate States of America, the conglomeration of Southern
states that seceded from the Union immediately before the
Civil War.

Young Jefferson did not enjoy school, and one day decided that he would no longer attend. His father accepted his decision, but told him that he could not simply stay at home and do nothing. Instead, he could go out into the cotton fields with the other workers. It took only two days before Jefferson decided that he would prefer to be back at school rather than out in the hot sun picking cotton.[2]

When he was nearly 14, Davis again left for boarding school, this time for Transylvania University in Lexington, Kentucky. He studied Latin, Greek, math, chemistry, physics, surveying, and public speaking. While he was away from home, his father died. Shortly before the elder Davis's death, he had arranged an appointment for Jefferson at West Point Military Academy in New York. Jefferson was hesitant. He thought that he might prefer to remain in the South and attend the University of Virginia, but finally he agreed to honor his father's wish and attend West Point.

In 1824 Jefferson Davis began his studies at the military academy. Among his classmates was a man with whom he would find himself linked in the future: Robert E. Lee, who would become the commander of the Confederate Army. Though Davis found that the military education suited him, he did have some trouble with authority at West Point. He was arrested and court-martialed in 1825 for drinking at a local pub, but he successfully defended his actions and the charges were dismissed. On December 25, 1826, he was again arrested and confined to quarters for what records describe as an "Eggnog Riot." He was released a few weeks later and graduated in 1828, twenty-third in a class of 33.

MILITARY CAREER

Davis was made a second lieutenant in the U.S. Army, and spent the next seven years serving at various posts in Missouri and Illinois, and in what was then called Iowa Territory, Wisconsin Territory, and Indian Territory. He was promoted to first lieutenant in 1833, and won the approval of his commanding officer, Colonel Zachary Taylor. At the time, the greatest conflict the army faced was with Native Americans. When the great Chief Black Hawk was finally captured, Colonel Taylor gave Jefferson Davis the responsibility for escorting the chief from Wisconsin to St. Louis.

Taylor may have trusted Davis with a Native American chief, but not, apparently, with his daughter. When Jefferson Davis met Taylor's daughter, 16-year-old Sarah Knox Taylor, he quickly fell in love. Despite her father's disapproval, Davis asked Sarah to marry him. He wrote to her on December 16, 1834, while stationed at Fort Bison in Arkansas Territory: "Sarah whatever I may be hereafter I will ascribe to you. Neglected by you I should be worse than nothing and if the few good qualities I possess shall under your smiles yield a fruit it will be yours as the grain is the husbandman's."[3]

With his future father-in-law strongly opposing the marriage, Davis at first decided to challenge Colonel Taylor to a duel, and then determined that the best course of action was for Davis to resign his military commission. He chose the latter course and married Sarah Knox Taylor on June 17, 1835, near Louisville, Kentucky, and then took his bride home to Mississippi. Once there, his oldest brother presented him with the 800 acres that Davis would name Brierfield. The couple did not have long to enjoy their marriage, though. Less than three months after their wedding, they both became seriously ill with malaria. On September 15, Sarah died. Davis survived and traveled to Cuba, where many sick Americans traveled at the time to regain their health and strength.

Davis eventually returned to Brierfield, determined to focus on his career as a farmer. He also developed an interest in local and state politics. Issues such as the antislavery movement and questions about tariffs were beginning to spark political debate. Davis's friends were impressed by his passionate arguments and thoughtful debates on the issues of the day, and they urged him to seek political office. In 1844 he was chosen as one of his state's Democratic presidential electors (an official who casts an electoral ballot in presidential elections). In December of that year, he cast his electoral vote for James K. Polk.

Around that time, his oldest brother introduced him to a friend's daughter, Varina Banks Howell. On February 26, 1845, Davis married Varina at the home of her parents in Natchez, Mississippi. He was 36, and she was only 18. They spent a happy honeymoon in New Orleans, and shortly after they returned to Brierfield, Davis was elected to the state's House of Representatives. The outbreak of war with Mexico in 1846 brought a quick end to his time in the state legislature: Davis resigned his office to serve as the head of the 1st Mississippi Regiment. This volunteer regiment, under Davis's leadership, became highly trained. They fought successfully under the higher command of Zachary Taylor, and by the time Davis was wounded and returned home, he was being praised as a military hero. He had earned the gratitude of Taylor, who told him, "My daughter, sir, was a better judge of men than I was."[4] He had also earned the admiration of Mississippi's governor, who appointed him to the U.S. Senate. (At that time, voters did not elect senators.)

A DEEPENING DIVIDE

Davis was outspoken in the U.S. Senate. He took pride in his experience, knowledge of military matters, and his unwillingness to compromise. Increasingly, debates in the Senate focused on the growing divide between the Northern and Southern states. Davis became a leader in the Senate and one of the most prominent advocates of what was called "Southern nationalism." This was not a position supporting independence or secession, but instead an argument for Southern influence within the United States.

The Mexican–American War had played an important role in this movement. After the war, significant territory in the South had become part of the United States—territory that would eventually become Texas, Arizona, New Mexico, Nevada, Utah, part of Colorado, and California (where gold had recently been discovered). At one point, the Midwest had been the focus of growth and development. Now that focus was on the southwestern portion of the United States.

In 1850, Davis spoke in the Senate against proposals to ban slavery in these newly acquired territories. This issue was causing intense debate among his colleagues and, indeed, among many Americans. Should slavery be made legal in these new additions to the United States, or should it be prohibited? That was the question sparking heated discussions. Slowly, a line was drawn across the once-united states, separating those states that permitted slavery from those that did not. Davis and many others saw it not simply as an issue of slavery, but of an entire way of life and of states' rights. In a debate in the Senate in January 1850, Davis stated, "We, sir, have not asked that slavery should be established in California. We have only asked that there should not be any restriction; that climate and soil should be left free to establish the institution or not, as experience should determine."[5]

Davis believed that Southern settlers should be free to move into the new territories with their slaves, and build homes and farms in these new lands. The effort to ban slavery in these territories was, he felt, an effort to prohibit Southern settlers from moving into these lands and claiming them as their own. The arguments he concentrated on were based on issues of states' rights and the Constitution. Even at this early date, Davis and others threatened secession should they lose this battle, a battle that at first focused on California.

Senator Henry Clay, proposed a compromise in which California would enter the Union as a free state and the issue of slavery in the other territories would be decided when they applied to be admitted to the United States. Most political leaders—and most Americans—were satisfied. War had been avoided. A sensible solution to the slavery question had been reached.

But Davis was outraged. He resigned his Senate seat in September 1851 and returned home to Mississippi, quickly entering the race for governor. He lost this race, just as he had lost the battle over slavery in the territories, and decided to give up politics permanently and focus on his cotton fields at Brierfield.

The election of Franklin Pierce as president would change Davis's fortunes yet again. Pierce had served with Davis during the Mexican–American War, and had been his friend in Congress. Pierce was no fan of the abolition movement (the movement to ban slavery), and he appointed Jefferson Davis as his secretary of war.

Davis left behind his threats of secession and focused instead on shaping the U.S. military into an elite fighting force. He renovated West Point, built up the army, and traveled extensively, particularly in the Northeast. He supported efforts to build the Pacific Railway through the South, to purchase additional territory from Mexico to further extend the railroad, and discussed the possibility of the U.S. annexation of Cuba.

In 1857 he returned to the Senate, where the divisions between North and South were once more sparking intense debate. Davis had stopped threatening secession, but his strong belief was that the future of the United States was in the South. As the secession movement began to sweep the South, many looked to Davis as their spokesman.

DIVIDING THE UNION

South Carolina was the first state to formally secede from the United States, doing so on December 20, 1860. Mississippi would soon follow, formally announcing its secession on January 9, 1861. It took nearly 11 days for the news to reach Mississippi's senator in Washington, and after learning of his state's decision, Davis knew that he needed to resign.

On January 21, 1861, five southern senators resigned from the U.S. Senate. Some were defiant. Robert Toombs of Georgia triumphantly declared, "Georgia is on the war path! We are as ready to fight now as we ever shall be. Treason? Bah!"[6]

Davis was more sober and sad than triumphant. "In the course of my service here, associated at different times with a great variety of Senators, I see now around me some with whom I have served long," he said, continuing:

> There have been points of collision; but whatever of offense there has been to me, I leave here; I carry with me no hostile remembrance. Whatever offense I have given which has not been redressed, or for which satisfaction has not been demanded, I have, Senators, in this hour of our parting, to offer you my apology for any pain which, in heat of discussion, I have inflicted. I go hence unencumbered of the remembrance of any injury received, and having discharged the duty of making the only reparation in my power for any injury offered. Mr. President, and Senators, having made the announcement which the occasion seemed to me to require, it only remains to me to bid you a final adieu.[7]

In the applause that followed, Davis simply returned to his seat, lowered his head, and covered his face with his hands. He had fought in too many battles to misunderstand what this conflict would mean. He still hoped that peace would be possible, but began to prepare for war.

So it was that Davis found himself in the rose garden of Brierfield in February 1861, waiting for the summons that would call him to begin the process of forming the Mississippi militia. He knew that other political leaders in the South were convening in Alabama to shape the new Confederate government, but Davis had had enough of politics. He believed that his greatest strengths were as a military officer, and felt that he could best serve the South in the war as a general.

On November 6, 1861, Jefferson Davis was elected president of the Confederacy. Having served as a military general before the secession, Davis took a personal interest in the Confederate military. Here, he poses with his staff in the field in May 1865.

When a messenger appeared with a telegram on that February 10, Davis thought that it might contain news about the militia or a request from the governor to report for duty. But the message was not what he expected. The telegram was dated February 9, and it was from Montgomery, Alabama:

Sir:

We are directed to inform you that you are this day unanimously elected President of the Provisional Government of the Confederate States of America, and to request you to

come to Montgomery immediately. We send also a special
messenger. Do not wait for him.

Varina Davis later recalled that her husband seemed deeply
distressed as he read the telegram. When he read it to her, she
said he spoke "as a man might speak of a sentence of death."[8]

Despite his distress, Davis understood the importance of
the task that lay before him. He above all stayed true to his
principles, believing his cause to be just and in need of defense.
He immediately packed his things and left for Alabama the
very next day—the same day, in fact, that the new president of
the United States, Abraham Lincoln, left Springfield, Illinois, to
attend his inauguration. As these two men moved toward their
respective destinies, their country prepared for war.

How Slavery
Shaped the Battle

The history of the United States has, from its earliest days, been intertwined with slavery. African slaves were brought to America well before Thomas Jefferson spoke of "liberty and justice for all." As early as the 1560s there were African slaves in the Spanish territory of Florida, and records show the sale of 20 slaves by a Dutch ship captain to English settlers in Jamestown, Virginia, in 1619.[1] Because the debate over slavery played such a critical role in the outbreak of the Civil War, it is important to briefly review the history of slavery in the United States, in order to understand its evolution and the strong emotions it inspired in both the North and South.

In the country's earliest days, slaves were brought in to provide labor for new settlements. The Dutch, who in the early seventeenth century settled the region that would ultimately become New York, brought many African slaves to their settlements along the Hudson River. In 1664, when the Dutch finally ended their rule over the area they called New Amsterdam, African slaves formed about 20 percent of the population of that territory. This did not end when the territory changed from Dutch to British hands. Some 100 years later, at least one-third of all physical labor in New York City was being performed by slaves.[2] The famous abolitionist Sojourner Truth was born a slave in Hurley, New York, around 1797 and would wait some 30 years before winning her freedom.

The North's distaste for slavery was a relatively recent phenomenon at the time of the Civil War: Slavery persisted in New York until 1827. Connecticut did not completely outlaw slavery until 1848.

Although the economy of the North was not dependent on slave labor in the way that the economy of the South was (with its focus on exports such as tobacco and cotton), slave labor still played a critical role in farming and early industries in the North. Slaves worked to build roads, clear the land, and herd cattle. They provided skilled labor—doing jobs such as shoemaking, blacksmithing, stone working, butchering, weaving, and carpentry. Slaves also served as dockworkers and sailors.

Slave ownership was an accepted practice in wealthy white households throughout the North. Scarcely 10 years before the signing of the Declaration of Independence in Philadelphia, three-quarters of that city's servant population consisted of black slaves.[3]

In Virginia, the majority of labor was initially provided by white servants in the early part of the seventeenth century, and it was only when this labor source began to dwindle that slaves were imported from Africa in significant numbers. In the late 1670s in Maryland and Virginia, white servants outnumbered black slaves 4 to 1. Not quite 20 years later, black slaves outnumbered white servants nearly 4 to 1.

The colony of Georgia was founded in the 1730s with the original idea that it would be a place for poor whites, as well as

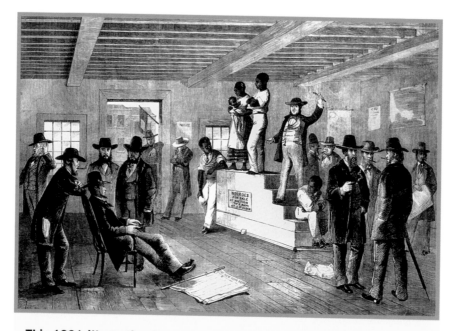

This 1861 illustration from the *Illustrated London News* depicts a slave auction taking place in Virginia. Although the debate over slavery is often cited as the cause of the Civil War, in fact it was not so clear-cut. Slavery was widely accepted in the North well into the nineteenth century.

orphans and debtors and those thought to be "unproductive." Its purpose was mainly to serve as a barrier between Spanish Florida and the British colony of South Carolina, but there was also the belief that Georgia could ultimately prove a source of products for export to England, products such as silk and wine. A law prohibiting slavery was passed in Georgia in 1735. This was due to a common belief that the presence of slaves might deter white workers from immigrating to Georgia. There was also a fear that the Spanish might use slaves to spark a rebellion. Georgia settlers finally asked for the repeal of the law in 1749 after the smuggling of numerous slaves into the territory and the desire of other settlers to obtain slave labor.

FREEDOM FOR SOME

In 1775, as the Revolutionary War began, slavery was legal in all of the American colonies. Thomas Jefferson wrote the words "all men are created equal," and yet was himself a slaveholder. Jefferson offers an interesting glimpse at the contradictions shown by the revolution leaders, who struggled to win their own independence from a "tyrannical ruler," and yet did not take concrete steps to eliminate the institution that prevented others in their country from also achieving their freedom.

Jefferson, like many of his fellow Virginia planters, spoke out in support of ending the slave trade in his early career in the Virginia Assembly and the federal Congress. It is important to note, however, that this was not an argument in favor of prohibiting slavery. It simply meant bringing an end to the practice of importing slaves from Africa. Slaves in the United States would remain. They would, in fact, become more valuable.

In Jefferson's initial draft of the Declaration of Independence, he included a passage blaming slavery and the slave trade on England's King George III. The Continental Congress ultimately deleted this. Still later, in the 1780s, Jefferson proposed more specific programs to address slavery. As a Virginia legislator, he believed that the state's economy and the prejudices of its citizens would not permit a total emancipation all at once of the approximately 200,000 slaves then in Virginia. Acting on this belief, Jefferson created a plan to gradually phase out slavery. In his plan, the children of all slaves born after 1800 would be considered free. They would be educated and, as adults, they would be settled in a community outside of Virginia where they would set up an independent society. Jefferson also proposed that slavery be prohibited in all of the territories of the West as a condition of their admission to the Union. Neither of these plans passed.

Despite these plans, Jefferson himself never took decisive action to free his own slaves. He made some provisions to free them upon his death, but when he died his estate was in debt and most of the slaves—viewed as part of his estate's "assets"— were sold.

Nonetheless, the language of the American Revolution did inspire a growing antislavery movement, particularly in New England. Pamphlets and sermons questioned the right of one human being to own another and decried the dehumanizing treatment of slaves. In 1777, as the Revolutionary War was under way, Vermont became the first colony—in fact, the first territory in the New World—to outlaw slavery. Massachusetts and New Hampshire followed in the early 1780s. In 1780, the Pennsylvania legislature adopted a law for the gradual emancipation of newborn children and descendants of slaves upon turning 28 years old. Slaves still appeared in the census of the state in 1830, though. In 1784 Rhode Island and Connecticut passed similar measures.

It took far longer for similar measures of gradual emancipation to succeed in states such as New York and New Jersey. Slavery was even more entrenched in Delaware and Maryland, although gradually the numbers of slaves decreased and the numbers of free blacks increased in both states. It was not until January 1, 1808, that the federal government finally outlawed the African slave trade. It would take the Civil War to finally settle the slavery question once and for all.

THE ABOLITION MOVEMENT

On March 4, 1858, James Henry Hammond, the governor of South Carolina, stood before the U.S. Senate and delivered a speech that clearly outlined the views of many Southerners by the mid-nineteenth century. In what became known as the "Cotton is King" speech, Hammond explained that slavery was a part of the natural order, an inevitable practice to ensure that the United States remained wealthy and a source of surplus production. Hammond stated:

In 1831, William Lloyd Garrison began publishing the *Liberator*, a weekly newspaper that focused on the abolition movement. With its strong language and often-controversial style, the *Liberator* became a centerpiece of the movement. The front page of the April 23, 1831 issue is shown here.

In all social systems there must be a class to do the menial duties, to perform the drudgery of life. That is, a class requiring but a low order of intellect and but little skill. Its requisites are vigor, docility, fidelity. Such a class you must have, or you would not have that other class which leads progress, civilization, and refinement. . . . Fortunately for the South, she found a race adapted to that purpose to her hand. A Race inferior to her own, but eminently qualified in temper, in vigor, in docility, in capacity to stand the climate, to answer all her purposes. We use them for our purpose, and call them slaves.[4]

I SELL THE SHADOW TO SUPPORT THE SUBSTANCE.

SOJOURNER TRUTH.

Sojourner Truth wears spectacles, a shawl, and a peaked cap in this portrait. Truth, who was born into slavery but escaped by running away, became an activist for abolition. For years, she traveled around the country, sharing her life story and campaigning for civil rights.

By the middle of the nineteenth century, the lines had been drawn between North and South, as Hammond's speech underscored. Slavery was becoming the issue around which both sides rallied. But what had transpired in the 100 years since the Revolutionary War to move slavery from being commonplace to a point of division between two sections of the United States?

There were critical moments: Eli Whitney's invention of the cotton gin in 1793 was one, setting the stage for the expansion of slavery in the South as cotton became a critical economic product for the region. From 1798 to 1808, more African slaves were brought into the United States than at any other time. Some 200,000 men and women were taken from Africa and sold into slavery during those 10 years. The Missouri Crisis of 1820 deepened the divide between Northerners and Southerners, as each side argued over the admission of new slave states to the Union. Throughout it all, voices echoed in the background arguing that a country founded on the principles of liberty and justice for all could not be a country that permitted slavery.

The gradual movement to abolish slavery began with a few courageous men and women who recognized the evils inherent in a system that allowed one group of people full domination over another. These abolitionists were regarded with disdain by their fellow citizens, criticized, and often physically attacked for their outspoken beliefs.

In 1833 the American Anti-Slavery Society was established, but the abolition movement actually began much earlier, well before the 13 colonies became the United States. Initially, arguments against slavery centered on certain religious groups, particularly the Quakers, also known as the Society of Friends. They used pamphlets and sermons to denounce the evils of slavery and later formed antislavery societies, and committees, published abolitionist newspapers, and sent representatives on lecture tours. Frequently, free blacks mobilized support for the antislavery movement and became leaders of the abolitionist movement.

The Quakers had abolished slavery among their members in 1776. In the latter part of the eighteenth century, Congregationalist minister Jonathan Edwards Jr., argued forcefully in his sermons against slavery in his sermons. Representatives from abolitionist societies in Connecticut, New York, New Jersey, Pennsylvania, Delaware, and Maryland gathered in Philadelphia

SOJOURNER TRUTH
(1797–1883)

Former Slave and Abolitionist

One of the country's earliest civil rights activists was a former slave named Sojourner Truth. She was born near Hurley, New York, around 1797, at a time when that area was Dutch territory. Her parents gave her the name Isabella, which she changed to Sojourner Truth when she was about 46 years old.

At the time of Truth's birth, slavery was well established in the New York area. It had existed for more than 150 years, since the time that Dutch settlers began enslaving Africans to work on their farms in the territory they called New Netherlands. The region became a British colony in 1664—a colony named New York—and the British continued the practice of importing more slaves.

At the age of 11, Truth was auctioned off to a storekeeper named John Nealy. At the time Truth spoke only Dutch, like her parents and former master. Her new master spoke only English, and frequently beat her, mainly because she could not understand in January 1794 and drafted a petition to Congress to prohibit the slave trade. They also sent appeals to the legislatures of the various states, urging them to abolish slavery.

Jim Pembroke, an escaped slave from Maryland, and David Walker, a free black, helped spearhead the African-American abolition movement in the late 1820s. Pembroke renamed himself James W.C. Pennington and became a prominent abolitionist. Walker published a radical pamphlet, *Appeal to the*

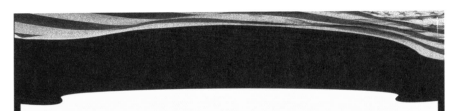

the orders she was given. She was sold several times as a young woman.

Truth married a fellow slave with whom she had five children. In 1826 she ran away to achieve freedom, carrying an infant daughter with her. She settled in New York City, as the state legislature had finally passed an emancipation law that all slaves born before July 4, 1799, would be freed by July 4, 1827.

Truth lived in New York until 1843, when she felt that God was calling her to leave New York City and become a traveling preacher. For several years she traveled throughout the East and Midwest, sharing her life story, speaking out against injustice, and working for women's rights and the abolition of slavery. She met many of the leading abolitionists of the day, and eventually published her own experiences in a book titled *The Narrative of Sojourner Truth, A Northern Slave*.

After the Civil War, Truth became active in the effort to assist former slaves, lobbying to secure for them land and money to relocate to the West. She died in Michigan in 1883.

Coloured Citizens of the World, which attacked slavery, evoking the American Revolution in its language. Walker was later killed outside his Boston shop.

As literacy and publishing increased throughout the states, abolitionist publications became a key component in the anti-slavery movement. On January 1, 1831, William Lloyd Garrison began publishing the *Liberator,* a weekly newspaper that focused on the abolition movement. Garrison believed that as a Christian, he had a duty to work to eliminate slavery. His paper, in strong language and often-controversial style, became a flashpoint for the movement.

The *Liberator* inspired yet another leading figure of the abolitionist movement. Frederick Douglass, an escaped slave, adopted Garrison as a mentor for a while, before setting off independently and founding his own abolitionist newspaper, *North Star.* His stated goal was the full abolition of slavery and the intellectual improvement of his enslaved countrymen. Douglas later became a prominent lecturer and abolitionist activist, meeting with Abraham Lincoln to offer his advice and perspective on the evils of slavery.

Despite these actions, it would take many years before the nation fully awakened to the evils of slavery. It is important to remember that an institution that provided prosperity and an easier lifestyle to some resulted in tremendous hardship and suffering to millions more. The men, women, and children who lived in bondage during the early years of U.S. history played a critical role in shaping the nation, and yet they knew little of freedom and justice. This inequality, this contradiction with the ideals on which the country was founded and the reality of life in the United States in the nineteenth century, helped slowly push the nation to the brink of war.

Laws Deepen
the Divide

Long before any shots were fired, deep divisions had appeared in the United States. Well-meaning political leaders had contributed to these divisions in an effort to respond to changes brought about in the nineteenth century. In some instances, laws were passed that were intended to hold the country together, but these laws instead emphasized how polarized the country had become.

In the early years after the United States had won its independence, the country was principally a nation of farmers. The South produced the nation's first president and many of the key revolution leaders. In 1800, the country was nearly evenly divided in population between North and South. Half of the 5 million people residing in the United States lived in the South. By 1850, however, only a third lived there, and only one of the nation's nine largest cities (New Orleans) was located in the lower South.[1]

This dramatic change in the first half of the nineteenth century was marked not only by rapid growth in the North, but also by a change in lifestyle, a change that highlighted the regional divide. In the North, manufacturing became an important source of income. Rapid growth led to more and more people living in towns and cities, rather than farms. Nine-tenths of the goods manufactured in the United States came from the North. The North began to grow not only in popula-tion, but in wealth as well.

The debate over slavery became a focal point for these grow-ing differences between Americans who claimed a Northern or Southern state as home. Increasingly, legislation marked this sharpening divide. As differences over economics, growth, and slavery grew entrenched, the new territories in the West became the stage on which the debate grew sharper and, eventually, vio-lent. As new states joined the Union, the issue of whether or not slavery would be allowed in those new states became a rallying point for those who believed their position was the right one.

As early as 1787, Congress had attempted to regulate not only settlement of territories in the West but also the policy toward slavery in those new lands. The Northwest Ordinance, passed by the Confederation Congress in 1787, had banned slavery north and west of the Ohio River. With the Louisiana Purchase of 1803, the size of the United States increased dra-matically, and the issue of whether or not slavery would be allowed in these new territories simmered until 1819, when the Missouri Territory applied for statehood.

Many Southerners had migrated into these new territories, bringing their slaves with them. What would their fate be? Should slavery be permitted in all of the new lands acquired in 1803, and if not, how would the question be resolved?

This was the issue facing congressional leaders when the petition from Missouri for statehood came up for vote in

Even before the Civil War, sharp differences marked the divide between North and South. In the South, agriculture remained the main industry, making that region more dependent on slave labor. Here, plantation laborers prepare to go to the field in 1862.

the House of Representatives. Congressman James Tallmadge of New York voiced the fears of many Northerners that the acceptance of slavery in these new territories would make the South far more powerful and influential. Tallmadge proposed an amendment to the statehood bill that would prohibit any further growth of slavery in Missouri and eventually set free the children of slaves in Missouri. The bill passed in the House but failed to pass in the Senate.

Eventually, a compromise was proposed to allow Missouri to join the Union. In this document, which would become known as the Missouri Compromise, Missouri would be admitted as a slave state. To balance this, a new state would be created out of the state of Massachusetts, which at that time reached northward all the way to the Canadian border. This

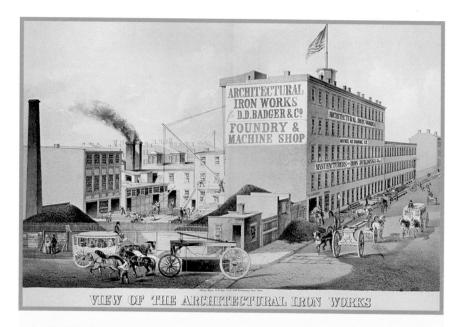

VIEW OF THE ARCHITECTURAL IRON WORKS

In the North, people flocked to cities to take part in the rapidly growing manufacturing industries. This foundry and machine shop in New York City is just one example of the new kinds of workplaces for those who wanted to get off the farm.

new state would become Maine, and slavery would be banned there. This ensured that the United States would be evenly divided into 12 states where slavery was permitted and 12 states where it was not.

In the new bill, Congress drew an imaginary line at 36 degrees 30 minutes north latitude through the Louisiana Purchase territory. In any territory lying above that line, slavery would not be allowed. The bill also noted that any slave escaping into any state of the United States or its territories could lawfully be reclaimed by his or her owner, regardless of whether or not the state of capture was considered a "free" state.

THE COMPROMISE OF 1850

In 1846, the United States went to war with Mexico. The war ended with the United States gaining millions of acres of new territory, most of it south of the line that had been drawn in the Missouri Compromise. Some 30 years had gone by since the Missouri bill had passed, and once again Congress found itself debating whether and where slavery should be permitted in this new western land.

Senators fiercely debated the issue, their position dictated by the state they represented. John C. Calhoun, a senator from South Carolina, argued fiercely that the Missouri Compromise had already settled the question: If the territory was south of the line, slavery was permitted there. Daniel Webster, a senator from Massachusetts, argued for a new compromise to resolve the question of slavery in the new territory. New York Senator William Henry Seward argued that slavery should not be permitted in any of the new territories because it was against what he called a "higher law"—in other words, a divine law that argued that slavery was evil.[2] With these heated debates came the first talk of Southern secession if the demands of the Southern states were not met.

Finally, after bitter discussions and a complicated series of proposals and counterproposals, the Compromise of 1850 passed. It reflected a number of issues: the discovery of gold in California in 1848, the increase in European immigration to the United States, and the growing number of Americans moving West. In the compromise, California was admitted to the Union as a free state. An ongoing dispute over borders between Texas and New Mexico was resolved with Texas being paid $10 million by the U.S. government to give up the disputed land and New Mexico and Utah being established as territories. The issue of slavery was resolved by allowing the population of each state to vote on whether or not it wanted slavery to be permitted there.

Within the Compromise of 1850 was also language that strengthened the law governing fugitive slaves. The new Fugitive Slave Act ordered federal marshals to assist in the capture of runaway slaves. If they did not, they would be fined $1,000.

Ordinary American citizens who helped a slave escape could be fined $2,000 or face six months in jail.

It was this act that proved troubling to those opposed to slavery, since it seemed to contradict the suggestion that each state could determine whether or not slavery would exist within its borders. A former congressman from Illinois named Abraham Lincoln reflected this confusion. "I confess, I hate to see the poor creatures hunted down," he said, "but I bite my lip and keep quiet."[3]

Others protested more vigorously, arguing that the Fugitive Slave Act made it clear that only the complete abolition of slavery would resolve the issue. In the early 1850s, Harriet Beecher Stowe's novel *Uncle Tom's Cabin* depicted how both white and black Americans were affected by the evils of slavery. The novel was initially published as a series in the antislavery journal *The National Era*, and was republished as a book in 1852. It became one of the best-selling books of the nineteenth century. Although most of the book was written in Maine—Stowe had spent only one weekend in a slave state—its moving depictions of the horrors of slavery and the tragic separation of families contributed to a new determination among many in the North that slavery must no longer be permitted in the United States.

BLEEDING KANSAS

By 1854, it was a debate over railroads that would help deepen the divide between North and South. Railroads had been non-existent when the Missouri Compromise of 1820 was drafted, but 34 years later railroads had become a principal means of carrying goods from one part of the country to another. Interest grew in the creation of a railroad that would cross the United States from coast to coast. Southerners insisted that the railroad must move along a southern route, but the North made the opposite argument.

The transcontinental railroad was a special issue for Senator Stephen Douglas of Illinois. If the railroad's hub were in

Chicago, it would bring great wealth to his state (and, perhaps not coincidentally, to himself through shrewd investments). But Southerners were lobbying hard for the central terminal to be located in the South, in St. Louis. In order for its hub to be in Chicago, the railroad would need to pass along a northern route, and Senator Douglas took every step to ensure that the northern route was the one chosen.

This ultimately involved yet another compromise, this time one that would ignore the Missouri Compromise of 1820. Douglas lobbied Northern and Southern colleagues in the Senate intensely, and the price ultimately paid for the northern railway was steep. Douglas's Southern colleagues insisted that settlers in Kansas and Nebraska would decide for themselves whether or not slavery would be allowed in their territories, and Douglas finally bowed to the pressure. If slavery were allowed into these territories, it would bring slavery north of the line determined by the Missouri Compromise of 1820. In effect, it would bring slavery into the North.

Douglas was able to win approval of his proposal from then-president Franklin Pierce. Through various compromises the bill passed both houses of Congress and became law on May 30, 1854. The bill seemed to ignite the strong passions that had been simmering below the surface. Nebraska was far enough north that few felt that slavery would flourish there. Kansas, on the other hand, was located next to the slave state of Missouri, and it was in Kansas that the war over slavery would begin in a period known as "Bleeding Kansas."

In March 1855, thousands of armed Missourians crossed the border from their state into Kansas territory. Kansas was to become the test for "popular sovereignty"—in this case, the policy that popular vote in an election would determine whether or not slavery was allowed in a state. Although the Compromise of 1850 had also applied popular sovereignty to New Mexico and Utah, those territories had not yet held legislative elections.

So it was in March 1855 that candidates presented themselves as either proslavery, abolitionist, or "Free State" (also known as Free Soil). The proslavery candidates wanted slavery to be legal in Kansas. The abolitionist candidates wanted slavery to be outlawed and for Kansas to be a safe haven for runaway slaves. The Free State/Free Soilers wanted slavery to be outlawed, but they wanted to take this process one step further, in banning all blacks—free or slave—from the territory.

Throughout the nation, the elections in Kansas were viewed as a test for the nation as a whole. Would the balance begin to shift toward slave states, or toward free states? To help stack the deck, representatives of both sides began sending their supporters to help settle the territory.

Rumors spread that 20,000 Northerners were coming into Kansas to cast their votes. It was for this reason that thousands of armed Missourians began crossing into Kansas shortly before the election. Voting in Kansas was open to "every free white male inhabitant above the age of 21 years who shall be an actual resident of said territory." The actual qualifications for a "resident" were broadly defined, and some of the Missourians claimed that they had become a resident that day, when they crossed the border. Carrying rifles, revolvers, knives, and wooden clubs, the Missourians bullied their way to the ballot boxes, and then cast their votes, determined that neighboring Kansas would become a slave state and not a safe haven for runaway slaves.

When the elections were announced, a total of 2,900 qualified voters resided in Kansas. Because of actions like those of the armed Missourians, more than 6,300 ballots were cast.[4] The proslavery votes carried the election by a wide margin and passed strict laws making it a crime to even speak against slavery. Antislavery opponents also moved into Kansas and attempted to set up their own abolitionist government in the territory. Violence erupted as these forces clashed. Shootings and stabbings routinely occurred, and a proslavery sheriff was murdered.

The violence spread beyond Kansas and onto the floor of the U.S. Senate. On May 19, 1856, Senator Charles Sumner of Massachusetts rose to his feet to denounce the steps that had been taken in Kansas, steps that would inevitably lead, he believed, to the territory becoming a slave state. He described the actions that had led to the adoption of slavery in Kansas as a "crime against nature, from which the soul recoils, and which language refuses to describe." He accused the South of being guilty of "a depraved longing for a new slave state, the hideous offspring of such a crime."[5]

For the rest of that day and on to the next, the senator continued his denunciation of slavery, the South, and any and all who supported what had happened in Kansas. His tirade included marked criticism of one of his fellow senators, Andrew Butler of South Carolina, a white-haired gentleman who happened to be absent from the Senate during Sumner's speech. "The senator touches nothing which he does not disfigure," Sumner stated in the conclusion of his lengthy tirade, "with error, sometimes of principle, sometimes of fact."[6]

The speech did not change any votes in the Senate. It reflected the passion that had spread beyond Kansas, that had spread beyond the Senate, and that was infecting the entire nation. As Sumner himself noted, the fight over Kansas would not merely be fought in the western territory, nor in the Senate, but would spread to a national stage "where every citizen will be not only spectator but actor."[7]

Even on the floor of the Senate, the time for debate and compromise was rapidly coming to an end. On May 22, after the Senate had adjourned for the day, Senator Sumner remained at his desk in the Senate chamber, working on some correspondence. A few senators were still at their desks, or chatting near the doorways, but the chamber was largely empty.

(continues on page 34)

THE CRIME AGAINST KANSAS

Brooks's attack on Sumner was sparked by Sumner's speech on May 19, 1856, denouncing the "Crime Against Kansas." A portion of that speech follows here:

. . . With regret, I come . . . upon the Senator from South Carolina (Mr. Butler), who, omnipresent in this debate, overflowed with rage at the simple suggestion that Kansas had applied for admission as a State and, with incoherent phrases, discharged the loose expectoration of his speech, now upon her representative, and then upon her people. There was no extravagance of the ancient parliamentary debate, which he did not repeat; nor was there any possible deviation from truth which he did not make, with so much of passion, I am glad to add, as to save him from the suspicion of intentional aberration. But the Senator touches nothing which he does not disfigure with error, sometimes of principle, sometimes of fact. He shows an incapacity of accuracy, whether in stating the Constitution, or in stating the law, whether in the details of statistics or the diversions of scholarship. He cannot open his mouth, but out there flies a blunder. . . .

But it is against the people of Kansas that the sensibilities of the Senator are particularly aroused. Coming, as he announces, "from a State" ay, sir, from South Carolina he turns with lordly disgust from this newly-formed community, which he will not recognize even as a " body politic." Pray, sir, by what title does he indulge in this egotism? Has he read the history of "the State" which he represents? He cannot surely have forgotten its shameful imbecility from Slavery, confessed throughout the Revolution, followed by its more shameful assumptions for Slavery since. He cannot have forgotten its wretched persistence in the slave-trade as the very apple of its eye, and the condition of its participation in the Union. He cannot have forgotten its constitution, which is Republican only in name, confirming power in the hands of the

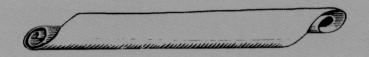

few, and founding the qualifications of its legislators on "a settled freehold estate and ten negroes." And yet the Senator, to whom that "State" has in part committed the guardianship of its good name, instead of moving, with backward treading steps, to cover its nakedness, rushes forward in the very ecstasy of madness, to expose it by provoking a comparison with Kansas. South Carolina is old; Kansas is young. South Carolina counts by centuries; where Kansas counts by years. But a beneficent example may be born in a day; and I venture to say, that against the two centuries of the older "State," may be already set the two years of trial, evolving corresponding virtue, in the younger community. In the one, is the long wail of Slavery; in the other, the hymns of Freedom. And if we glance at special achievements, it will be difficult to find any thing in the history of South Carolina which presents so much of heroic spirit in a heroic cause appears in that repulse of the Missouri invaders by the beleaguered town of Lawrence, where even the women gave their effective efforts to Freedom. . . . Were the whole history of South Carolina blotted out of existence, from its very beginning down to the day of the last election of the Senator to his present seat on this floor, civilization might lose—I do not say how little; but surely less than it has already gained by the example of Kansas, in its valiant struggle against oppression, and in the development of a new science of emigration. Already, in Lawrence alone, there are newspapers and schools, including a High School, and throughout this infant Territory there is more mature scholar-ship far, in proportion to its inhabitants, than in all South Carolina. Ah, sir, I tell the Senator that Kansas, welcomed as a free State, will be a "ministering angel" to the Republic, when South Caro-lina, in the cloak of darkness which she hugs, "lies howling." . . .

Source: Institute for Advanced Technology in the Humanities, www.iath.virginia.edu.

(continued from page 31)

Sumner became aware that a young man was standing beside him. The young man was Preston Brooks, a congressman from South Carolina and the nephew of Senator Butler. "I have read your speech twice over, carefully," Brooks said. "It is a libel on South Carolina and on Senator Butler, who is a relative of mine."[8] Brooks was carrying a cane, and he proceeded to lift the cane high in the air and then brought it down with all of his strength on Senator Sumner's head. He continued to beat Sumner and, when the cane broke from the force of his blows, he kept hitting him with the splintered remains until blood covered the senator's head and clothing.

The beating continued until several men ran to Sumner's aid. Brooks then walked calmly away, stating, "I did not intend to kill him, but I did intend to whip him."[9] Sumner did not return to the Senate for three years. His spine had been affected by the beating, and his speech and ability to walk were severely damaged. An attempt to expel Brooks from Congress failed to get enough votes, and many in the South hailed him as a hero. He received many canes as gifts to replace the one that had splintered on Sumner's head.

The blows Brooks struck were not simply the reflection of an enraged nephew who felt injury against his family's honor. They were evidence that the issues that were dividing the nation would inevitably lead to violence, and that when the representatives of the people were shedding blood on the floor of the U.S. Senate, all of the United States would soon be called to choose sides.

John Brown's Raid

On a Sunday evening, October 16, 1859, a tall, thin Ohio farmer led a small army into battle, hoping that he would not only strike a blow against slavery in Kansas but also inspire slaves throughout the United States to rush to join him and his abolitionist army. The farmer's name was John Brown, and 21 years before his fateful raid, he had vowed to destroy slavery. In his past were numerous business failings, and unsuccessful attempts at earning a living in six different states. Throughout the years, however, he had become convinced of one thing: that he was divinely appointed to bring an end to slavery. He managed, in the process, to convince others of this as well.

Brown's belief was that blood would need to be shed in order to bring an end to slavery, and he was willing to sacrifice his own and that of his four sons who had joined his army. Several famous abolitionists, including Frederick Douglass, had offered him secret support. (Douglass had, nonetheless, declined Brown's invitation to join his army.)

Two days after Senator Sumner had been beaten bloody in the Senate chamber, Brown—then living in Kansas—and seven men responded to the violence in Kansas with violence of their own. They crept through the ravines bordering Pottawatomie Creek in Kansas, armed with swords and determined to prove that it was not only slavery supporters who had a voice in Kansas. Their targets were any proslavery settlers living along the creek. When they came to a cabin, they ordered the men in the home to come out, quickly murdered them, and moved on to the next cabin. In all, five men were brutally killed that night before Brown and his group returned to their homes.

In January 1859, Brown went to Ontario, Canada, a region that had become home to many free blacks and escaped slaves fleeing the long reach of the Fugitive Slave Act. Brown urged them to return to the United States, asking them for their help in his effort to spark a revolution. In Brown's speech he promised more than a revolution. He said that he would help them carve out a new territory, with a constitution that would ban slavery. Brown declared that he would carry this constitution to all slaves in the South, oversee the revolution, and serve as the protector of this new territory as its commander in chief.[1]

On the evening of October 16, 1859, Brown led his army of 13 white men and 5 black men (including a few from Ontario) into the small village of Harpers Ferry, Virginia. To help spark his revolution, Brown brought with him a wagon containing 200 rifles, 200 pistols, and 1,000 pikes (long spears). Brown was convinced that the local slaves would quickly join his cause, so he had brought along all of these weapons for those who would rise up when they saw his army.

There was a federal armory located at Harpers Ferry, and Brown and his men soon took control of it, as well as the

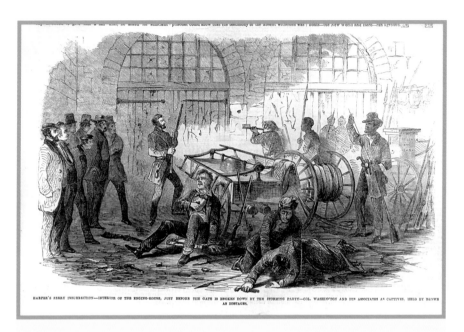

HARPER'S FERRY INSURRECTION—INTERIOR OF THE ENGINE-HOUSE, JUST BEFORE THE GATE IS BROKEN DOWN BY THE STORMING PARTY—COL. WASHINGTON AND HIS ASSOCIATES AS CAPTIVES, HELD BY BROWN AS HOSTAGES.

In 1859, abolitionist John Brown selected Harpers Ferry as the target for a raid in which he planned to seize the munitions and ignite a revolution that would end slavery. This etching depicts a scene in which Brown holds hostages in the Engine House during the raid.

arsenal and engine house. Hostages were taken, including the great-grandnephew of George Washington.

Brown's plans soon began to fail, though. The first man his army killed was not a slavery supporter, but was instead a free black man who happened to be the town baggage master. Brown's group came under attack. The first of his men to die was a former slave who had planned, by joining Brown's army, to ultimately free his wife and children from the Virginia plantation where they were slaves.[2] Nine more of Brown's men were killed in the fight, including two of his sons.

Passengers on a train traveling through Harpers Ferry saw the fighting between Brown's men and the angry townspeople. The alarm carried to Washington, D.C., where 90 U.S. Marines were quickly placed under the command of Lieutenant Colonel

Robert E. Lee of Virginia and hurried to Harpers Ferry. Brown and his men had taken refuge in the engine house when the Marines arrived. The Marines used sledgehammers and an improvised battering ram to break through the doors. In the scuffle, Brown received a serious sword wound before he and his men were captured.

A treason trial was quickly arranged in Virginia, and held while Brown was still too weak from his wounds to defend himself or even to sit up. He was found guilty and sentenced to death by hanging. The execution took place at Charles Town, guarded by some 1,500 troops. On the morning of Brown's hanging, writer Henry Wadsworth Longfellow noted in his diary that the date "will be a great day in our history, the day of a new Revolution—quite as much needed as the old one."[3]

In the heated atmosphere of those years leading up to war, Brown was proclaimed a martyr by many abolitionists, although there were some who wisely noted that Brown's mission was suicidal and his plans insane. In the South, any words of praise for Brown seemed to underscore the deepening divide within the nation. Fears of a slave rebellion were fanned by word of Brown's ambitions, and white Southerners began to arm themselves for battle.

John Brown's raid on Harpers Ferry would prove to be yet another decisive step on the path to the Civil War. Brown reportedly never spoke before his hanging, but he did hand a note to one of his guards: "I, John Brown, am now quite certain that the crimes of this guilty land will never be purged away but with Blood."[4]

THE *DRED SCOTT* DECISION

The turmoil in Kansas and the question of slavery led to violence in many other places where the slavery issue inspired fierce emotions. Finally, the slavery question landed before the U.S. Supreme Court in the case of *Dred Scott v. Sandford*.

Dred Scott marks one of the most shameful instances of attempts to legally respond to the question of slavery in the United States. Dred Scott was a slave who had been taken by his master, an army surgeon, into the state of Illinois and the territory of Wisconsin, both of which banned slavery. Eventually, Scott moved into the slave state of Missouri and was sold by his master to John F.A. Sanford. (The court misspelled Sanford's name as *Sandford* in its final written decision, and the misspelling stands to this day in court documents.) Scott ultimately sued for his freedom, arguing that, because slavery was outlawed in the free territory and state where he had lived for a time, he had become a free man there.

The argument was initially supported by the Circuit Court of St. Louis, and then overruled by the Missouri Supreme Court. With the support of several prominent white abolitionists, Scott managed to get his case into federal court. There the argument changed: The case now became about whether a slave had the legal right to sue in a federal court.

The case ultimately made its way to the U.S. Supreme Court, where the court had first to decide whether Scott had the legal right to sue in federal court. If not, the federal court had no jurisdiction, or right, to rule on the matter at all. If the court did have jurisdiction, the justices could then decide on Scott's claim for freedom.

The chief justice of the Supreme Court, Roger B. Taney, was a strong supporter of slavery. Like many Americans of the time, he too had strong feelings about the growing divide between North and South. In his view, the North was intent on forcing its views on those in the South, and he felt it his duty to protect Southerners from what he viewed as Northern aggression.

In March 1857, the court ruled that, because Scott was a slave, he was not entitled to the rights of a free citizen to

(continues on page 43)

DRED SCOTT V. SANDFORD

In 1857, the U.S. Supreme Court ruled in the case of *Dred Scott v. Sandford* that a black man could never become a citizen, and that Congress had no power to prohibit slavery in any of the federal territories. The case would eventually be overturned by the passage of the Thirteenth and Fourteenth Amendments to the Constitution, but its startling language reveals the powerful sentiments at work in the United States prior to the Civil War, as these excerpts reveal:

> In the opinion of the court, the legislation and histories of the times, and the language used in the Declaration of Independence, show that neither the class of persons who had been imported as slaves, nor their descendants, whether they had become free or not, were then acknowledged as a part of the people, nor intended to be included in the general words used in that memorable instrument.
>
> It is difficult at this day to realize the state of public opinion in relation to that unfortunate race, which prevailed in the civilized and enlightened portions of the world at the time of the Declaration of Independence, and when the Constitution of the United States was framed and adopted. But the public history of every European nation displays it in a manner too plain to be mistaken.
>
> They had for more than a century before been regarded as beings of an inferior order, and altogether unfit to associate with the white race, either in social or political relations; and so far inferior, that they had no rights which the white man was bound to respect; and that the negro might justly and lawfully be reduced to slavery for his benefit. He was bought and sold, and treated as an ordinary article of merchandise and traffic, whenever a profit could be made by it. This opinion was at that time fixed and universal in the civilized portion of the white race. It

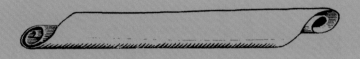

was regarded as an axiom in morals as well as in politics, which
no one thought of disputing, or supposed to be open to dispute;
and men in every grade and position in society daily and habitu-
ally acted upon it in their private pursuits, as well as in matters
of public concern; without doubting for a moment the correctness
of this opinion. . . .

Now, as we have already said in an earlier part of this
opinion, upon a different point, the right of property in a slave is
distinctly and expressly affirmed in the Constitution. The right to
traffic in it, like an ordinary article of merchandise and property,
was guaranteed to the citizens of the United States, in every
State that might desire it, for twenty years. And the Government
in express terms is pledged To protect it in all future time, if the
slave escapes from his owner. This is done in plain words—too
plain to be misunderstood. And no word can be found in the
Constitution which gives Congress a greater power over slave
property, or which entitles property of that kind to less protection
than property of any other description. The only power conferred
is the power coupled with the duty of guarding and protecting the
owner in his rights.

Upon these considerations, it is the opinion of the court that
the act of Congress which prohibited a citizen from holding and
owning property of this kind in the territory of the United States
north of the line therein mentioned, is not warranted by the Constitution, and is therefore void; and that neither Dred Scott himself, nor any of his family, were made free by being carried into
this territory; even if they had been carried there by the owner,
with the intention of becoming a permanent resident.

*Source: "100 Milestone Documents," http://www.ourdocuments.gov
(U.S. National Archives and Records Administration)*

JAMES BUCHANAN,

FIFTEENTH PRESIDENT OF THE UNITED STATES.

The decision in *Dred Scott v. Sandford* caused a split within the powerful Democratic Party. President James Buchanan (above), who gained much of his support from the South, supported the decision. In fact, there is some evidence that Buchanan persuaded one of the Supreme Court justices to vote in favor of the ruling.

(continued from page 39)

sue in federal court. Writing for the majority opinion, Chief Justice Taney referred to the framers of the Constitution who, he wrote, believed that blacks "had no rights which the white man was bound to respect; and that the negro might justly and lawfully be reduced to slavery for his benefit. He was bought and sold and treated as an ordinary article of merchandise and traffic, whenever profit could be made by it."[5] In the court's opinion, slaves were not, and never could be, citizens.

That should have ended the court's involvement, but the justices went further. Chief Justice Taney stated that territories could never bar slavery, because doing so deprived slaveholders of their property. Taney also stated that Congress had no power to prohibit slavery in any of the federal territories. This ruling essentially marked the Missouri Compromise of 1820 as unconstitutional: Congress could not forbid citizens from taking slaves (described as "property") into any U.S. territory.

Dred Scott marked one of the lowest moments in Supreme Court history. Charles Evans Hughes, who later served as chief justice, described it as a "self-inflicted wound."[6] While Southerners cheered the ruling, it sparked protest not only among abolitionists, but also throughout the North. The decision even caused a split within the powerful Democratic Party. Newly elected President James Buchanan, who gained much of his support from the South, supported the decision. In fact, there is some evidence that Buchanan persuaded one of the Supreme Court justices to vote in favor of the ruling.[7] Another leading Democrat, Senator Stephen Douglas, was furious at the decision and openly criticized Buchanan's alleged involvement.

This divide in the powerful Democratic Party reflected the division within the country as a whole. It also presented an opportunity for a new political party to step into the void. That party was the recently formed Republican Party, and their candidate, Abraham Lincoln, would take advantage of the situation to rise to the presidency three years later.

Party Politics

The United States in the 1850s was a nation increasingly marked by differences and disagreements over how the country should set policy. It is not surprising that the nation's political parties reflected these differences.

In the years leading up to the Civil War, political parties played a key role in elections. The parties were strong, marked by clear and very different positions on major issues. Voters tended to be very loyal to their party. Political parties were a part of family identity, with a son supporting the party his father had supported. (Women did not yet have the right to vote.) A man's political party revealed much about his social status, his position in society, and his economic class.

From the 1820s to the 1850s, two political parties dominated the country: the Democratic Party and the Whig Party. The Democrats dominated most presidential elections, winning three of the five presidential elections between 1836 and 1852, and modeling their candidates after Andrew Jackson, the highly popular Democratic president, who served from 1829 to 1837.

But beginning in the 1850s, the changes impacting the country as a whole began to be felt by both the Democratic Party and the Whig Party, as different factions began to emerge, especially in the North. Prejudice against foreigners, as large numbers of German and Irish immigrants came to the United States, and also against Catholics (as many of these new immigrants followed Catholicism) led to the formation of some smaller political groups.

Slavery was yet another point of division. The Democratic Party had strong support in the South. The party's role in the Kansas-Nebraska Act that favored opening Kansas to settlement by slave owners led some Northern antislavery groups to break away from the party, calling themselves anti-Nebraska Democrats.

The Whig Party gradually weakened to the point of near collapse, and former Whigs and members of the antislavery Democratic faction began to look for a new party that would more fully represent their views. There were many smaller parties catering to these anti-Catholic, Free Soil, and antislavery viewpoints. The Republican Party, however, rapidly became the large party that unified all these groups under a single party label.

By 1860, 14 of the 18 governors in the Northern United States were Republicans. The party dominated all but 3 of the state legislatures in the North, and 102 of the 146 Northern seats in the U.S. House of Representatives were in Republican hands.

TRIUMPH OF THE REPUBLICAN PARTY

The Republican Party, founded in Wisconsin in 1854, first rose to power at the local and state levels. Its founders included

This is a campaign banner for the Whig Party, which existed from 1834 to 1854 and was formed in opposition to President Andrew Jackson. The Compromise of 1850 on the issue of slavery split the party; Southern Whigs defected to the Democratic Party while Northern Whigs joined the newly formed Republican Party in 1854.

former Whigs and Democrats and its platform focused on opposition to the spread of slavery into Kansas and Nebraska. Among the former Whigs who chose to join the Republican

Party when the Whig Party collapsed was a former legislator from Illinois named Abraham Lincoln.

In 1856, the Republican Party held its first presidential convention in Philadelphia, nominating John C. Frémont, a leading figure in the exploration of the West. The campaign called on Congress to ban slavery in the western territories. The party slogan was "Free labor, free speech, free men, free Kansas, and Frémont."

For a new national party, the Republicans did surprisingly well, carrying 11 states in the North and winning two-fifths of the electoral votes. As the 1860 presidential election neared, leading Republicans began to speculate on who would be their nominee. The convention was held in Chicago at the suggestion of the secretary of the Republican National Committee, Norman Judd, who also happened to be a friend of Abraham Lincoln's. Judd arranged for the majority of the seats at the convention to be given to Chicagoans, who loudly cheered, screamed, and whistled when the name of "their candidate"—Abraham Lincoln—was put into nomination.

Lincoln had been viewed as, at best, a possible candidate for vice president. He had spent only two years serving at the national level in Congress, and had risen to prominence as a result of a series of debates with Stephen Douglas in a Senate campaign—a campaign Lincoln had lost. But as a result of his "local" support at the convention, he was suddenly taken more seriously. Through negotiations at the convention by his supporters (Lincoln himself was not at the convention), he became the eventual nominee.

In the 1860 election, the Democratic Party was so fiercely divided by the slavery issue that Northern and Southern divisions of the party nominated different candidates for the presidency. In the South, John C. Breckenridge was the Democratic nominee for the presidency, while the Northern wing nominated Stephen Douglas as their candidate.

JOHN C. FRÉMONT

In 1856, the Republican Party held its first presidential convention in Philadelphia, nominating John C. Frémont, who had been a leading figure in the exploration of the West. The slogan was "Free labor, free speech, free men, free Kansas, and Frémont."

With the Democratic Party running different candidates in different parts of the country, a Republican victory became almost inevitable. Lincoln received only 40 percent of the popular vote but captured the presidency with 60 percent of the electoral votes.

THE RISE OF LINCOLN

The presidential election of 1860 was one of the most significant in U.S. history, marked by such bitter and intense debate that the fate of the country seemed to depend on the outcome. The disintegration of the Democratic Party into separate geographic wings seemed to inevitably point to a victory by the Republican candidate, Abraham Lincoln. Democratic leaders in the South had vowed to lead their states in a move to secede the Union if Lincoln won. On the morning after the election, the editor of the *Illinois State Register* wrote in an editorial, "The election of Mr. Lincoln will be a national calamity."[1] He did not yet know the election results, but the collapse of the Union that followed seemed to prove the truth of his words.

The nation's sixteenth president is now regularly cited as one of its greatest, but it is important to remember that many in both the North and South viewed his election in 1860 with great dismay. Many people correctly believed that his election would prove the final blow to the Union, the "last straw" that would spark Southern states to secede. An editorial in the *York Democratic Press* of York, Pennsylvania, published on November 13, 1860, noted, "Lincoln and Hamlin, the sectional candidates of the Black Republican party, have been elected President and Vice-President of the United States by a decided majority. It is useless to speculate upon the result, but it is . . . humiliating to every conservative and union-loving man in the country."[2]

Note that these two newspapers with their criticism of Lincoln's election were both Northern newspapers. In the South, the dismay was even greater. One example is the following editorial from the New Orleans *Daily Crescent* of November 13, 1860:

(continues on page 52)

A HOUSE DIVIDED

On June 16, 1858, the Illinois Republican Party held its state convention in the Springfield Hall of Representatives. Abraham Lincoln was the unanimous choice of the Republican state convention to run against Stephen Douglas for the Senate seat. Lincoln read a speech (excerpted below), reflecting his dismay with the *Dred Scott* decision in the Supreme Court and the reasons why the Republican Party rose over the divisive issue of slavery.

"A house divided against itself cannot stand." I believe this government cannot endure permanently half slave and half free. I do not expect the Union to be dissolved—I do not expect the house to fall—but I do expect it will cease to be divided. It will become all one thing, or all the other. Either the opponents of slavery will arrest the further spread of it, and place it where the public mind shall rest in the belief that it is in the course of ultimate extinction; or its advocates will push it forward till it shall become alike lawful in all the States, old as well as new, North as well as South. . . .

Two years ago the Republicans of the nation mustered over thirteen-hundred thousand strong. We did this under the single impulse of resistance to a common danger, with every external circumstance against us. Of strange, discordant, and even hostile elements, we gathered from the four winds, and formed and fought the battle through, under the constant hot fire of a disciplined, proud, and pampered enemy. Did we brave all then to falter now?—now, when that same enemy is wavering, dissevered, and belligerent? The result is not doubtful. We shall not fail—if we stand firm, we shall not fail. Wise counsels may accelerate or mistakes delay it, but, sooner or later, the victory is sure to come.

Source: *Philip Van Doren Stern, ed.,* The Life and Writings of Abraham Lincoln *(New York: Modern Library, 1940), pp. 429, 437–438.*

Stephen Douglas served two terms in the House of Representatives before he was elected to the Senate in 1846. Douglas was also a leading contender for the Democratic presidential nomination in 1852 and 1856. In 1858, Abraham Lincoln challenged Douglas to a series of seven debates in Illinois as a part of Lincoln's campaign to unseat Douglas as the U.S. senator from Illinois.

(continued from page 49)

The history of the Abolition or Black Republican party of the North is a history of repeated injuries and usurpations, all having in direct object the establishment of absolute tyranny over the slave-holding States. . . . They have robbed us of our property, they have murdered our citizens while endeavoring to reclaim that property by lawful means, they have set at naught the decrees of the Supreme Court, they have invaded our States and killed our citizens, they have declared their unalterable determination to exclude us altogether from the Territories, they have nullified the laws of Congress, and finally they have capped the mighty pyramid of unfraternal enormities by electing Abraham Lincoln to the Chief Magistracy, on a platform and by a system which indicates nothing but the subjugation of the South and the complete ruin of her social, political, and industrial institutions.[3]

Step by step, inevitably, the country had moved toward hatred not of some external force or foreign aggression, but of one way of life that was different from another. It was hatred of one state for another, hatred of one American for another. On December 4, 1860, Senator Alfred Iverson of Georgia delivered a speech to his fellow senators, declaring, "There is an enmity between the northern and southern people that is deep and enduring, and you never can eradicate it—never! You sit upon your side, silent and gloomy; we sit upon ours with knit brows and portentous scowls. . . . We are enemies as much as if we were hostile States."[4]

Abraham Lincoln

There were many in the South who celebrated when word reached them that Abraham Lincoln had been elected president. They believed that the last obstacle to secession had been removed, and that it was now clear that the South must strike for its independence.

William Boyce, a U.S. congressman from South Carolina, reportedly gave a stirring speech before a crowd of secessionists in Charleston while waiting for the election results. "I think the only policy for us is to arm as soon as we receive authentic intelligence of the election of Lincoln," he said. "It is for South Carolina, in the quickest manner, and by the most direct means, to withdraw from the Union. Then we will not submit, whether the other Southern States will act with us or with our enemies."[1]

The man whose election marked the final breaking point in the once-united states was born into poverty and seemed to have risen to the presidency by chance and because of the divisions within the Democratic Party. Lincoln's father, Thomas, had come from Virginia and spent time in New Jersey and Pennsylvania before moving to Kentucky, where he built a one-room, dirt-floor cabin in the wilderness. A few months after the cabin was built, Abraham Lincoln was born, in February 1809. The family eventually moved to Indiana, where Lincoln's mother died when he was nine. His father remarried, choosing a widow with three children. Thomas Lincoln's new wife loved her stepson and insisted that he get an education, whether briefly at school or more often through studying at home. When he didn't have a slate to write on, he used a board of wood, shaving it with a knife as a makeshift eraser.

Abraham Lincoln grew tall and thin and, as a young man, took a job as a deckhand on a flatboat traveling to New Orleans. When he returned at age 21, he joined his family on a move to central Illinois. There, he and a cousin were hired to split 4,000 rails for their neighbors. This would form the core of his political biography: a Western man from the frontier who had grown up in poverty and worked splitting rails. He worked as a store clerk, and then joined a debating society. In 1832, he became a candidate for the state legislature, but he instead enlisted in the Illinois militia and was elected captain. In the autobiographical sketch he prepared for his campaign biography in June 1860, he said that no other success in his life gave him as much satisfaction.[2]

His company fought in no battles, and he returned after nearly two months to resume his campaign for the legislature with only two weeks remaining until the election. His first political speech was at a country auction, where the 23-year-old candidate appeared in a frayed straw hat and calico shirt, his pants held up by a single suspender.[3] "If elected, I shall be thankful," he said, "if not, it will be all the same."[4]

Lincoln lost, and took on a series of jobs, working splitting rails, in a grocery store, as a postmaster, and studying surveying and law. In 1834 he ran again for the legislature and won, serving four terms there. He was licensed as a lawyer in 1836, and would eventually become a partner in a Springfield law firm and a respected trial lawyer. In 1842 he married Mary Todd from Kentucky, with whom he would have four sons. Mary Todd had grown up in a slaveholding family.

Lincoln, at the time a member of the Whig Party, was defeated in runs for the U.S. Congress in 1842 and 1844. He finally won a congressional seat in 1847, but his opposition to the war with Mexico cost him his seat two years later. For the five years that followed, Lincoln focused on his law practice. It was the Kansas-Nebraska Act, supported by Senator Stephen Douglas of Illinois, that finally brought Lincoln out of political retirement.

THE LINCOLN-DOUGLAS DEBATES

When Senator Douglas returned to his home state, he found many who opposed his efforts on the Kansas-Nebraska Act. Among them was Abraham Lincoln, who in Springfield invited Douglas to a speech in which Lincoln outlined his disagreements with Douglas's bill.

Douglas had tried to focus attention on the idea of "popular sovereignty," or states' rights, but for Lincoln the bill was about slavery. "Slavery is founded in the selfishness of man's nature, opposition to it in his love of justice," Lincoln said. "Repeal the Missouri Compromise, repeal all compromises; repeal the Declaration of Independence, repeal all past history—you still cannot repeal human nature. It still will be in the abundance of man's heart that slavery extension is wrong, and out of the abundance of his heart his mouth will continue to speak."[5]

Lincoln was reelected to the legislature, failed at a run for the U.S. Senate, and in 1856 was nearly nominated as vice president on the Republican presidential ticket with John C.

Frémont. In 1857, he decided to challenge Douglas for his Senate seat. He invited Douglas to participate in a series of debates in each of seven congressional districts.

These debates would make Lincoln nationally famous. The *Dred Scott* decision by the Supreme Court and slavery in the territories in the West became the focus of the debates. "Let us discard all this quibbling about this man and the other man—this race and that race and the other race being inferior, and therefore they must be placed in an inferior position. . . . Let us discard all these things, and unite as one people throughout this land, until we shall once more stand up declaring that all men are created equal," Lincoln said at one debate.[6] Lincoln urged the Illinois audiences to take a position and declare the spread of slavery to be wrong. He warned them against attempting to assume a false neutrality on the issue, as he accused Douglas of doing.

Douglas won the senatorial election by a slim majority, but Lincoln began looking ahead almost immediately. "The cause of civil liberty must not be surrendered at the end of *one*, or even, *one hundred* defeats," he told one disappointed supporter.[7]

PATH TO THE PRESIDENCY

Abraham Lincoln's presidential nomination was the result of savvy manipulation by supporters, and his election was at least partly a result of a split in the Democratic Party. He did not campaign; it was considered undignified. Lincoln and his opponents each claimed to be best suited to preserve the Union. There were ultimately four candidates for the presidency in 1860: Lincoln on the Republican ticket, Stephen Douglas and John Breckinridge as the Northern and Southern Democratic nominees, respectively, and John Bell of the newly formed Constitutional Union Party. Lincoln won only 40 percent of the popular vote—his name did not even appear on the ballots in 10 Southern states—but he won 180 electoral votes, a clear majority. Breckinridge won 72, Bell 39, and Douglas 12.

COPYRIGHT 1908
BY
niasVolk

One of the most recognizable faces in American politics, Abraham Lincoln made history as the sixteenth president of the United States. In a speech before his inauguration, Lincoln pledged: "So long, then, as it is possible that the prosperity and liberties of this people can be preserved within this Union, it shall be my purpose at all times to preserve it." In the four months between Lincoln's election and his inauguration, however, the Union began to dissolve.

The headlines in the *New York Times* on the day after the election declared the results, and hinted at the future. "Astounding Triumph of Republicanism," read one. "The North Rising in Indignation at the Menaces of the South,"[8] read another. The Southern states had threatened to secede if Lincoln was elected, and there was much anxiety in the days following his triumph. He did little to soothe these worries in the weeks before his inauguration, instead joking about his decision to grow a beard, or speaking of the need for patience.

There was pressure on Lincoln to emphasize his moderate views to the South, perhaps to visit a slave state, or to appoint a Southerner to his cabinet. But overall, Lincoln kept silent. He was not yet president—James Buchanan was still in office— and it is possible that Lincoln viewed the talk of secession as the threats of a small group of radicals. In a speech in New York before his inauguration, Lincoln did emphasize his determination to hold the country together: "So long, then, as it is possible that the prosperity and liberties of this people can be preserved within this Union, it shall be my purpose at all times to preserve it."[9] In the four months between Lincoln's election and his inauguration, however, the Union he had sworn to preserve began to dissolve. South Carolina was the first to secede, and six more states soon followed.

On February 11, 1861, 52-year-old Lincoln left Springfield. He would never return. For 12 days he slowly made his way to Washington, stopping in five states for speeches, appearances, and meetings. Baltimore was the last scheduled stop on his roundabout journey, but before his arrival there, Lincoln learned of a plot to kidnap or assassinate him before he reached Washington. Lincoln was persuaded to pass by Baltimore without stopping, and to slip quietly into Washington before dawn, without fanfare. Many in the South rejoiced at this embarrassing beginning of Lincoln's presidency. Lincoln was caricatured in Southern papers as a prairie bumpkin, a coward, slipping furtively into Washington in a plaid cap and long black cloak.

LINCOLN'S INAUGURAL ADDRESS

On March 4, 1861, Lincoln took the oath of office before a crowd of thousands next to a Capitol building that was still under construction. Sharpshooters stood nearby, and riflemen, artillery, and cavalry all watched for would-be attackers. The country was on the eve of its greatest crisis, but Lincoln in his inaugural address spoke of his determination to hold together the Union:

> Apprehension seems to exist among the people of the Southern States, that by the accession of a Republican Administration, their property, and their peace, and personal security, are to be endangered. There has never been any reasonable cause for such apprehension. Indeed, the most ample evidence to the contrary has all the while existed, and been open to their inspection. It is found in nearly all the published speeches of him who now addresses you. I do but quote from one of the speeches when I declare that "I have no purpose, directly or indirectly, to interfere with the institution of slavery in the States where it exists. I believe I have no lawful right to do so, and I have no inclination to do so." . . .
>
> In your hands, my dissatisfied fellow country men, and not in mine, is the momentous issue of civil war. The government will not assail you. You can have no conflict, without being yourself the aggressors. You have no oath registered in Heaven to destroy the government, while I shall have the most solemn one to "preserve, protect, and defend" it. . . .

Source: Roy P. Basler, ed., The Collected Works of Abraham Lincoln, Vol. 4 (New Brunswick, N.J.: Rutgers University Press, 1953), pp. 262–263, 271.

On February 22, 1861, the *Montgomery Post* of Alabama summed up the South's disgust with the new president of the United States:

The more we see and hear of his outgivings on the way to Washington, the more we are forced to the conclusion that he is not even a man of ordinary capacity. He assumes to be insensible of the difficulties before him—treats the most startling political questions with childish simplicity, and manifests much of the disposition of the mad fanatic who meets his fate—not in the spirit of respectful Christian resignation, but with the insane smile of derision upon his lips, as if unconscious of the destiny that awaits him.[10]

The United States Ceases to Exist

The formal separation of the United States of America began in South Carolina, under the leadership of William H. Gist, its governor. Gist, a lawyer and a planter, suspected well before the 1860 election reached its end that Lincoln would be victorious. He wrote letters to governors of other states in the South, urging them to form a unified front.

Gist told his fellow governors that South Carolina would hold a state convention if and when Lincoln's election became official. If any other states chose to secede, South Carolina would join them. If no other state seceded immediately, then South Carolina would be the first to leave the Union.

The governors sent back very different replies. The governors of North Carolina and Louisiana explained that their people had not yet made up their minds, and that the election of a Republican president would probably not be enough to convince them to leave the Union. The governors of Mississippi and Alabama suggested that a meeting of the slave states might be necessary before any action was taken. The governor of Georgia said that he would call for a convention of the state's people to determine how the state should act. The governor of Florida also called for a state convention, noting that his state would not take the lead in secession "but will most assuredly cooperate with or follow the lead of any single Cotton State which may secede."[1]

It seemed that most of the states in the South were waiting on the edge of secession, waiting for something more than the election of a Republican president to determine their future. They were largely unified in their shared interests and in their sense of the perceived wrongs that had been done to them, and would come together if one state took the lead.

That state was South Carolina. On October 12, Governor Gist called the legislature of South Carolina into special session to name the state's presidential electors—a routine procedure. On this occasion, however, Gist told the legislators that he felt that they should remain in session until the election results were final. If Lincoln won, he recommended that a state convention be ordered: a convention whose mission would be to pass a declaration of secession.

When the results were announced, the city of Charleston, South Carolina, celebrated with the same kind of joy as the people of Springfield, Illinois. In Springfield, they celebrated the election of their native son, Lincoln. In Charleston, they celebrated with flags and fireworks and booming cannons the fact that a new nation was being created, and the creation was taking place in Charleston. The state's two U.S. senators submitted their resignations from federal office.

In December 1860, 170 men in South Carolina came together in a state convention that would ultimately determine the fate of the United States. The men had, for the most part, determined to secede by the time they gathered in the state

The cover for this sheet music shows one of the official flags of the Confederate States of America, though other flags would be flown on the battlefield.

capital of Columbia, and they believed that the rest of the South would follow their lead. Because smallpox was spreading through Columbia, the delegates voted to reconvene in Charleston, where they arrived on December 18 to a large parade.

On December 20, South Carolina unanimously adopted an Ordinance of Secession. The state's "Declaration of the Causes of Secession" concluded with the phrase that formally brought an end to the Union that had held the states together for nearly 100 years:

> We, therefore, the people of South Carolina . . . have solemnly declared that the Union heretofore existing between this State and the other States of North America is dissolved, and that the State of South Carolina has resumed her position among the nations of the world, as a separate and independent State, with full power to levy war, conclude peace, contract alliances, establish commerce, and to do all other acts and things which independent States may of right do.[2]

For two days the delegates joined the city in celebration, but then they met again to determine what steps now had to be taken. One focus was on the military forts that the U.S. government had built and maintained in South Carolina, including Fort Johnson, Fort Moultrie, Castle Pinckney, and the still-incomplete Fort Sumter. The convention decided that these forts belonged to South Carolina, and that a committee of three men should be charged with the task of traveling to Washington to negotiate with the U.S. government for their transfer.

The delegates also outlined in a formal document the causes for secession, a document intended for the people of the United States. A second document was also produced. This one, addressed to "the People of the Slave-holding States of the United States," was intended to point out the injustices of the U.S. government and persuade slave-holding states to join the people of South Carolina in secession. The document stated:

All fraternity of feeling between the North and the South is lost, or has been converted into hate; and we, of the South, are at last driven together by the stern destiny which controls the existence of nations. United together, we must be the most independent as we are the most important of the nations of the world. United together, and we require no other instrument to conquer peace than our beneficent productions. United together and we must be a great, free, and prosperous people, whose renown must spread through the civilized world, and pass down, we trust, to the remotest ages. We ask you to join us in forming a Confederacy of Slave-holding States.[3]

There was no real talk of war in this document, no strong sense that violence would inevitably follow the secession of states, or that hundreds of thousands of young men would lose their lives in battle. But war would soon follow.

South Carolina's talk of seizing control of the forts, and its efforts to more fully arm its militia, sparked concern among the U.S. officers in control of military outposts in South Carolina. Many of these men were Southerners, and their loyalty would be tested should an attempt be made to take the forts by force. The forts were thinly staffed, and Fort Sumter had only the workmen who were attempting to complete its construction. Five days after South Carolina formally seceded, the few federal troops (some 82 men) still stationed at Fort Moultrie, in the midst of sand dunes on South Carolina's coast, were moved to Fort Sumter. Fort Moultrie was located amidst a group of summer cottages. It was believed that Fort Sumter, further out in the harbor, would keep the troops safe and, in their commander's words, "prevent the effusion of blood."[4]

On January 9, 1861, Mississippi decided to secede from the United States. Florida seceded the next day. Alabama, Georgia, and Louisiana followed. Texas Governor Sam Houston attempted to stop his state from joining the Confederacy. Instead, he was forced out of office, and Texas left the United States. "Let me tell

Texas Governor Sam Houston (above) attempted to stop his state from joining the Confederacy. Instead, he was forced out of office, and Texas left the United States.

you what is coming," Governor Houston warned. "Your fathers and husbands, your sons and brothers, will be herded at the point of the bayonet. . . . You may, after the sacrifice of countless millions of treasure and hundreds of thousands of lives, as a bare possibility, win Southern independence. . . . But I doubt it."[5]

LEADING A NATION

On February 11, 1861, two men set out from their hometowns to become president. One was Abraham Lincoln. The other was Jefferson Davis.

Davis had learned of his election as president of the provisional government of the Confederate States of America only the day before. He had held no real political ambitions in this new government. Instead, he had hoped to lead an army if war would come.

The government Davis had been chosen to lead had a constitution very similar to that of the United States, but there were a few important differences. The Confederate Constitution specifically granted the right to own slaves. The president would serve for a single six-year term and would not be eligible for reelection. Each member of his cabinet would also serve in the Confederate Congress. The new nation's capital would be in Montgomery, Alabama.

As Lincoln began his slow and roundabout route to Washington in preparation for his inauguration, Davis traveled by train to Montgomery. The train stopped along the route, giving people the opportunity to see their new president and greet him with cheers. Davis cautioned in his speeches what few others had said: that the decision to secede would mean war, and they should prepare for it to be a long one.

Davis reached the new capital on the evening of February 17, and the following day he took his oath of office on the steps of Montgomery's state capitol building. It was an impressive ceremony: Davis rode to the capitol in a carriage pulled by six matching gray horses as part of a parade, with uniformed militia and cannons firing salutes before a crowd of some 10,000 people.

Davis had never been a leader in the charge for secession. He had been chosen, in part for this very reason—for his moderate positions, and for his reputation as a senator and a military man. Seven states had joined the Confederacy, but

Virginia—the most populous state in the South and the birth-place of seven American presidents—had still not joined, nor had the border states. Davis was meant to reassure them, and in his inaugural speech he did.

He did not speak of slavery but instead, of agriculture and of justice, using terms that invoked Thomas Jefferson at the time of the Revolutionary War. Davis said:

> It is joyous in the midst of perilous times to look around upon a people united in heart, where one purpose of high resolve animates and actuates the whole, where the sacrifices to be made are not weighed in the balance against honor and right and liberty and equality. Obstacles may retard, but they cannot long prevent the progress of a movement sanctified by its justice and sustained by a virtuous people. Reverently let us invoke the God of our fathers to guide and protect us in our efforts to perpetuate the principles which by His blessing they were able to vindicate, establish, and transmit to their posterity. With the continuance of His favor, ever gratefully acknowledged, we may hopefully look forward to success, to peace, and to prosperity.[6]

Alexander H. Stephens of Georgia had been chosen as the vice president of the provisional government of the Confederacy, for similar reasons as Davis. Stephens had unsuccessfully argued in the Georgia legislature to hold off from secession. He had been chosen as vice president mainly as a way to appease Georgians who had wanted their candidate, Howell Cobb, to be the Confederacy's president. But after taking the oath of office as the Vice President of the Confederacy, Stephens was far more blunt than Davis had been: "Our new government is founded on the opposite idea of the equality of the races. . . . Its corner stone rests upon the great truth that the Negro is not equal to the white man. This . . . government is the first in the history of the world based upon this great physical and moral truth."[7]

Davis was eager to promote unity among the seven states that had voted to secede, and as a result his cabinet contained one man from each of these states. These men were not, for the most part, the leaders of the secession movement. In fact, all of them, at least at one point in their lives, had been supporters of the United States. Three had been born outside the United States. Davis was not closely acquainted with any of them. Two of the men he did not know at all, but they had been recommended to him by political advisers.

The cabinet included Robert Toombs of Georgia as secretary of state, Christopher Memminger of South Carolina as secretary of the treasury, and Leroy Pope Walker of Alabama as secretary of war. Stephen Russell Mallory of Florida was appointed secretary of the navy, and John H. Reagan of Texas was appointed postmaster general. Serving as attorney general was former senator Judah P. Benjamin of Louisiana.

In this group, Davis was clearly the most prominent and politically powerful. The Confederacy would have a strong executive branch, and it would speak with a single voice—that of Jefferson Davis. In the Union, Abraham Lincoln would try a very different experiment. His cabinet would contain many of the most outspoken political leaders in the nation, several of them his former opponents.

There was a necessarily makeshift air about the Confederate government at the beginning. The first meeting of the cabinet was held in a hotel room, with a piece of paper pinned to the door indicating which one was the president's office. The secretary of the treasury was forced to buy his own desk and chair, and the task of printing the first Confederate money was given to a New York company since there was no adequate printing press in the South. A visitor to the new capital encountered Confederate Secretary of State Robert Toombs, and asked him for the location of the State Department. "In my hat, sir," Toombs replied, "and the archives in my coat pocket."[8]

Davis was convinced that war would follow, and he determined to prepare for it. At his urging, the Confederate Congress empowered him to summon and use the states' militia, and later to provide for a Confederate army, which would be composed not only of these militia but also at least 100,000 volunteers. A general staff was established for this army. Also,

DECLARATION OF THE CAUSES OF SECESSION

On December 20, 1860, South Carolina became the first Southern state to vote to secede. The convention later issued a "Declaration of the Causes of Secession," from which this excerpt is taken:

. . . We affirm that . . . [the] ends for which this Government was instituted have been defeated, and the Government itself has been destructive of them by the action of the non-slaveholding States. Those States have assumed the right of deciding upon the propriety of our domestic institutions; and have denied the rights of property established in fifteen of the States and recognized by the Constitution; they have denounced as sinful the institution of Slavery; they have permitted the open establishment among them of societies, whose avowed object is to disturb the peace of and eloin [remove] the property of the citizens of other States. They have encouraged and assisted thousands of our slaves to leave their homes; and those who remain, have been incited by emissaries, books, and pictures, to servile insurrection. . . .

On the 4th of March next . . . a party will take possession of the Government. It has announced that the South shall be excluded from the common territory, that the Judicial tribunal a Committee on Naval Affairs was formed and directed to consider building ironclad frigates and gunboats. Regulations were passed to determine what ranks would be given to those officers who had formerly served in the U.S. Army. A national flag was designed and was raised over the Montgomery capitol building on March 4, 1861. There were now two capitals in what had once been the United States, two constitutions, two presidents, and two armies.

shall be made sectional, and that a war must be waged against Slavery until it shall cease throughout the United States.

The guarantees of the Constitution will then no longer exist; the equal rights of the States will be lost. The Slaveholding States will no longer have the power of self-government, or self-protection, and the Federal Government will have become their enemy. . . .

We, therefore, the people of South Carolina, by our delegates in Convention assembled, appealing to the Supreme Judge of the world for the rectitude of our intentions, have solemnly declared that the Union heretofore existing between this State and the other States of North America is dissolved, and that the State of South Carolina has resumed her position among the nations of the world, as a separate and independent State, with full power to levy war, conclude peace, contract alliances, establish commerce, and to do all other acts and things which independent States may of right do.

Source: Kenneth M. Stampp, ed., The Causes of the Civil War *(Englewood Cliffs, N.J.: Prentice-Hall, 1959), p. 37.*

Fort Sumter

On February 25, 1861, President Jefferson Davis appointed three commissioners to travel to Washington. Their task was to negotiate for the surrender of federal forts and other federal installations (lighthouses and arsenals, for example) in the territory of the Confederate states. The men represented different viewpoints and different states—A.B. Roman of Louisiana, Martin J. Crawford of Georgia, and John Forsyth of Alabama. Davis charged his commissioners with an important task: They were to carry a friendly message to Washington to ask for things to which the Confederacy believed it was rightfully entitled.

In Davis's account of his experiences in the Confederacy, *The Rise and Fall of the Confederate Government*, published in 1881, he wrote of having sent these commissioners in some haste to Washington to meet with President Buchanan before

Lincoln would take office. "I had received an intimation from him through a distinguished Senator of one of the border states [Senator Hunter of Virginia], that he would be happy to receive a Commissioner or Commissioners from the Confederate States, and would refer to the Senate any communication that might be made," Davis explained.[1]

The commissioners had apparently believed that they would be received cordially, and that negotiations would begin immediately to formalize the terms of the separation between their new nation and the United States. But President Buchanan, with only a few days remaining in his presidency, refused to meet with them. The commissioners were alarmed at the hatred of many in the city when their arrival became known.

Within Confederate territory there were four federal forts still flying the Union flag, and it was these forts that soon became the focus of efforts by the commissioners and those who were opposed to their mission. The four were Fort Sumter in Charleston Harbor, and three others in Florida: Fort Pickens in Pensacola Bay, Fort Taylor at Key West, and Fort Jefferson in the Dry Tortugas.

Fort Sumter's situation had become the most critical. Prior to South Carolina's secession, the fort had only been staffed by the workers attempting to complete it. These workers arrived by boat in the morning and then left in the evening when their work was finished. Shortly after secession was announced, Major Robert Anderson of the United States had evacuated his 82 men from Fort Moultrie to Fort Sumter, believing that Sumter's position three miles out in the harbor was safer and easier to secure. Officials in South Carolina had protested this move. President Buchanan responded by sending an unarmed ship with men and supplies to reinforce the fort.

The unarmed ship quickly came under fire as it sailed into Charleston, and the ship turned back. Buchanan took no further action, so the situation when the commissioners arrived

THE GREAT FIGHT AT CHARLESTON S.C. APRIL, 7TH 1863

Fort Sumter was the site of the Battle of the Ironclads, as Union forces unsuccessfully attempted to recapture the fort.

in Washington, just as Lincoln was preparing to assume the presidency, was tense. The harbor at Charleston was ringed with men whose guns were kept trained on Fort Sumter. The Union soldiers stationed there were no longer allowed to leave the fort to buy food and supplies. On the day after Lincoln's inauguration, a message for him arrived in Washington. Major Anderson reported that supplies at Fort Sumter were running low. There was not enough food to last more than six weeks.

NEGOTIATIONS AND DEALS

One of Lincoln's first decisions as president was how to respond to the situation at Fort Sumter. The commissioners were still in Washington. They attempted to meet with Lincoln, but he refused to see them, as did his secretary of state, William H. Seward. Seward had little confidence in Lincoln, however, and determined to do some behind-the-scenes negotiation in an effort to prevent the nation from slipping into civil war. Seward was worried about the growing tension, worried that Fort Sumter would become the tipping point that would push the nation over the brink. He was convinced that with proper consideration and negotiation, the states that had seceded would ultimately return to the Union.[2]

Seward could not openly meet with the commissioners, but he could meet with a justice of the Supreme Court. So, on March 15, as Lincoln met with his cabinet to discuss the response to Fort Sumter, Justice John Campbell entered Seward's office. Campbell was from Alabama but he had not yet returned to the South since the secession. He had come to Seward to persuade him to meet with the commissioners. Seward refused, and in doing so made a startling statement—that within three days Lincoln would order the evacuation of Fort Sumter. It was precisely what the commissioners were hoping to achieve.

As this message was carried back to the Confederacy, Lincoln sent three men of his own to Charleston to report back first-hand on the situation there. Two reported that the situation was impossible. The third suggested that it might be possible to reinforce the fort with supplies and men.

While the status of Fort Sumter remained in question, a state convention was taking place in Virginia. At the convention, the delegates had voted against leaving the Union but were still in session. Lincoln, through one of the delegates, offered a proposal: If the convention would adjourn immediately, with the vote against secession standing, he would evacuate Fort Sumter. "A state for a fort is no bad business," he said.[3]

This deal was never finalized, and Lincoln continued to seek the advice of his cabinet on the question of the fort. Most felt that the fort should not be relieved. Some, including Seward, argued that the fort was too close to Washington. They said that if a stand was going to be taken over any fort it should be Fort Pickens in Florida.

On April 1, Justice Campbell returned to Seward to ask him what had happened to the plans to evacuate Fort Sumter. Seward replied that, if Lincoln did decide to send supply reinforcements to the fort, he would certainly notify South Carolina's governor first. This was, of course, quite different from Seward's previous message. When word of this change in position reached the Confederacy, the blame for this apparent deception was placed not on Seward but on Lincoln, since it was believed that Seward was speaking on behalf of Lincoln's administration.

UNDER SIEGE

There was tremendous sympathy in the North for the help-less soldiers at Fort Sumter as their fate was decided. The *New York Times* urged, "The Administration must have a policy of action. Better almost anything than additional suspense. The people want *something* to be decided on [to] serve as a rallying point for the abundant but discouraged loyalty of the American heart."[4]

The man in charge of the fort, Major Anderson, was a career soldier from Kentucky. He had once owned slaves him-self, and was sympathetic to the Southern cause, but he had taken an oath to faithfully serve his country and he intended to honor that oath to the best of his ability.

By April 6, Lincoln had made his final decision. He had sworn to protect and preserve the Union, and Fort Sumter would be where his efforts would begin. He contacted the governor of South Carolina and told him that he would send supplies to Fort Sumter but would not attempt to reinforce it with more soldiers or weapons, provided that neither the fort nor the fleet carrying the supplies was attacked. When word of Lincoln's decision reached the Confederate government, Jefferson Davis was confronted with a difficult choice: They could either back down from their threats, or fire the first shot in what was certain to be war (and that first shot would be fired to prevent hungry men from getting food).

Davis consulted his cabinet. One member strongly warned that firing on Fort Sumter would launch a civil war. "Mr. President, at this time it is suicide, murder, and you will lose us every friend at the North," he said. "You will wantonly strike a hornets' nest which extends from mountains to ocean. Legions now quiet will swarm out and sting us to death. It is unnecessary; it puts us in the wrong; it is fatal."[5]

As the presidents made their decisions, the men inside and outside Fort Sumter maintained their positions, following the procedures of their commanders. These were men who, in some cases, had served together in military units. Many of their leaders had trained together at the U.S. Military Academy at West Point. Until recently they had all been Americans. Now they found themselves facing the possibility of killing each other.

When mistakes were made—when guns accidentally went off or were fired in the wrong direction—the commanders exchanged polite notes of apology, notes which were responded to with equally polite replies. The requests from Major Anderson to officials in Charleston to allow his men access to food were formal and gracious. The Confederate officials' polite refusals echoed this courteous tone. At one point Major Anderson's wife arrived from New York and persuaded the governor of South Carolina to allow her to visit her husband. A Confederate boat carried her to the fort, where she was able to spend a brief visit with her husband before safely being carried away by the Confederate boat.

FINAL DECISION

There were many who advised Davis not to respond with hostility to Lincoln's effort to supply Fort Sumter, but Davis ultimately believed that Lincoln had deceived him, and that the

(continues on page 80)

FORT SUMTER IS OCCUPIED

In his *Rise and Fall of the Confederate Government*, Jefferson Davis includes many documents outlining the Confederacy's position in the time leading up to the Civil War. One of these is the following letter, sent on December 28, 1860, from the commissioners of South Carolina to President James Buchanan. The letter was sent shortly after South Carolina had seceded and Major Anderson had moved his men from Fort Moultrie to Fort Sumter:

> SIR: We have the honor to transmit to you a copy of the full powers from the Convention of the People of South Carolina, under which we are "authorized and empowered to treat with the Government of the United States for the delivery of the forts, magazines, lighthouses, and other real estate, with their appurtenances, within the limits of South Carolina, and also for a division of all other property held by the Government of the United States as agent of the confederated States of which South Carolina was recently a member; and generally to negotiate as to all other measures and arrangements proper to be made and adopted in the existing relation of the parties, and for the continuance of peace and amity between this Commonwealth and the Government at Washington."
>
> In the execution of this trust, it is our duty to furnish you, as we now do, with an official copy of the ordinance of secession, by which the State of South Carolina has resumed the powers she delegated to the Government of the United States, and has declared her perfect sovereignty and independence.
>
> It would also have been our duty to have informed you that we were ready to negotiate with you upon all such questions as are necessarily raised by the adoption of this ordinance, and that we were prepared to enter upon this negotiation with the earnest

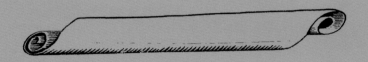

desire to avoid all unnecessary and hostile collision, and so to inaugurate our new relations as to secure mutual respect, general advantage, and a future of good-will and harmony beneficial to all the parties concerned.

But the events of the last twenty-four hours render such an assurance impossible. We came here the representatives of an authority which could, at any time, within the past sixty days, have taken possession of the forts in Charleston Harbor, but which, upon pledges given in a manner that, we can not doubt, determined to trust to your honor rather than to its own power. Since our arrival here an officer of the United States, acting, as we are assured, not only without but against your orders, has dismantled one fort and occupied another, thus altering, to a most important extent, the condition of affairs upon which we came.

Until these circumstances are explained in a manner which relieves us of all doubt as to the spirit in which these negotiations shall be conducted, we are forced to suspend all discussion as to any arrangements by which our mutual interests might be amicably adjusted.

And, in conclusion, we would urge upon you the immediate withdrawal of the troops from the harbor of Charleston. Under present circumstances, they are a standing menace which renders negotiation impossible, and, as our recent experience shows, threatens speedily to bring to a bloody issue questions which ought to be settled with temperance and judgment.

Source: Jefferson Davis, The Rise and Fall of the Confederate Government, *Vol. 1, reprint edition (New York: Thomas Yoseloff, 1958), pp. 591–592.*

(continued from page 77)

world would know that he had been forced into action. Many years later, in his *Rise and Fall of the Confederate Government,* Davis still vigorously defended his decision:

> The attempt to represent us as the *aggressors* in the conflict which ensued is as unfounded as the complaint made by the wolf against the lamb in the familiar fable. He who makes the assault is not necessarily he that strikes the first blow or fires the first gun. To have awaited further strengthening of their position by land and naval forces, with hostile purpose now declared, for the sake of having them "fire the first gun," would have been as unwise as it would be to hesitate to strike down the arm of the assailant, who levels a deadly weapon at one's breast, until he has actually fired.[6]

Davis's decision was undoubtedly influenced by the status of the Virginia convention, still in session. Some suggested that an attack on Fort Sumter would help persuade Virginia to join the Confederacy. Supporting this idea was Congressman Roger Pryor of Virginia, who addressed a cheering crowd in Charleston, "If you want us to join you, *strike a blow!*"[7]

Davis issued a message through his secretary of war to General P.G.T. Beauregard, commander of the defenses of Charleston Harbor and a man who had been taught artillery at West Point by the very man he was now guarding—Major Anderson. The message instructed Beauregard that Washington intended to supply Fort Sumter, so he should immediately demand its evacuation or, if this was refused, "proceed in such manner as you may determine to reduce it."[8]

Shortly after midnight on April 12, 1861, Beauregard dispatched two Confederate ambassadors to the fort. They were rowed out to the fort, their boat carrying a white flag. Beauregard's message to his former teacher was respectful as he requested the fort's evacuation: "All proper facilities will be

Major Robert Anderson, the commanding officer at Fort Sumter, refused to surrender the fort to the Confederacy. Upon his refusal, at 4:30 A.M. on April 12, 1861, the Civil War began.

afforded for the removal of yourself and command, together with company arms and property, and all private property, to any post in the United States which you may select. The flag which you have upheld so long and with so much fortitude, under the most trying circumstances, may be saluted by you on taking it down."[9]

Anderson read the message sadly. He considered himself a Southerner, born in Kentucky and married to a woman from Georgia. Kentucky had not yet decided whether or not to secede, though, and he had sworn an oath to serve the United States. He replied to Beauregard that he regretted his inability to comply with the request, noting to the two Confederate agents that, in any event, those in the fort would starve to death in only a few more days.

Once more Beauregard ordered the boat to return to Fort Sumter, this time with four Confederate agents and a more specific message: If Anderson did not surrender by 4 A.M.—in one hour—the fort would be fired upon. Anderson replied that he did not intend to surrender, and then shook the hands of each of the four men as he escorted them back to their boat. "If we never meet in this world again," he said, "God grant that we may meet in the next."[10]

The ambassadors carried their message back and the order was given to fire. One of the men was Richard Pryor, the Virginia congressman who two days earlier had urged those in Charleston to "strike a blow." He was offered the honor of firing the first shot on Fort Sumter, but he quickly refused. Instead it was another Virginian, a 67-year-old secessionist named Edmund Ruffin, who fired first.

It was 4:30 A.M. on April 12, 1861. The Civil War had begun.

A Nation at War

The siege at Fort Sumter lasted only 34 hours. Major Robert Anderson finally surrendered. He asked for and was allowed to take with him the American flag, now shredded by gunfire, as he and his troops sailed north.

The war that followed the gunfire at Fort Sumter would last longer—nearly four years longer. It began with the fall of Fort Sumter and ended with the Confederate Army's surrender near Appomattox Court House in Virginia on April 9, 1865. Those four years would dramatically impact the country and alter the nation that resulted from that conflict.

On April 14, 1865, Major Robert Anderson would once again stand at the flagpole at Fort Sumter. The fort was now little more than a shell, severely damaged by two years of bombardments by the Union in an effort to recapture Sumter from Confederate hands. It was the fourth anniversary of the surrender at Fort Sumter, and Major Anderson produced the ragged flag he had carried away from the fort when it was surrendered.

Before an audience of dignitaries from the North and some 4,000 freed slaves, Anderson spoke, at first hoarse with emotion and then more clearly. "I thank God I have lived to see this day," he said.[1] Only a few hours after Anderson raised the tattered flag over the remains of Fort Sumter, John Wilkes Booth slipped into President Lincoln's box at the Ford Theatre in Washington and shot him. Lincoln would die the following morning.

VICTORIES AND DEFEATS

Immediately after news of the fall of the fort reached Washington, President Lincoln called upon the governors of the states and territories to supply him with an army of volunteers. The call was for 75,000 militiamen, each told that their time of service would be 90 days. Men rushed from all parts of the country to volunteer for "their" army, and both the Union and Confederate armies were flooded with volunteers in those early days of the war.

When Virginia voted to secede—five days after the fall of Fort Sumter—the capital of the Confederate states was moved to Richmond. Tennessee, Arkansas, and North Carolina quickly followed Virginia in leaving the Union. The nation was thus divided between 11 Confederate states and 23 Union states.

The Union had an advantage not only in number of states, but in population as well. As the war began, there were some 21 million people living in the North, compared with only 9 million in the Confederate states. Of that 9 million, 3.5 million were slaves whose masters did not dare provide them with weapons to fight.

The first major clash between the two armies took place in July near Manassas Junction, Virginia, only 25 miles from Washington, D.C. Many people from Washington, excited at

Civil War soldiers were often lacking in supplies, including matching uniforms, as shown in this photo.

the prospect of the war's first major battle, rode out in carriages from the city, bringing picnic baskets and binoculars. The Confederate Army had formed an eight-mile line along one side of Bull Run Creek and there they awaited the advancing Union forces.

The battle seesawed back and forth between the two armies, until the Confederate Army ordered a fierce counterattack accompanied with high-pitched yells (which would come to be known as the "rebel yell"). They forced the Union into a retreat, joined in their panic by the Washingtonians who had come to witness the battle. The battle would be known as Bull Run in the North and Manassas in the South. Some 4,500 men would be killed, wounded, or captured.

Lincoln responded to this defeat by calling for an additional 100,000 troops. They would now be serving for three years instead of three months. It was clear that this war would not be short-lived and would claim many lives.

LETTER FROM A CONFEDERATE SOLDIER

D.C. Snyder was a Virginian soldier with the Confederate Army during the Civil War. He wrote several letters to his wife while serving, detailing army life and how he missed his family and friends. In this letter, he encouraged his wife not to give up hope:

My Dear Wife,

About an hour since I rec'd your kind Letter written at "Milton Valley," 26th ulto, and mailed at Luray Jan'y 3rd. I was truly glad to hear from you dear Rachel for I have thought so much of you today from some cause. Not withstanding I have been busy writing all day yet thoughts of home and the dear ones there would continually flit across my mind. I took a long walk just before dark and ascended a steep hill where I took a seat and surveyed the country around and conversed in thought with you and the dear little ones. . . .

You seem to be very despondent and think "the South is nearly done." But while I admit that everything is apparently dark and not very encouraging, yet my dear Rachel "the South is not nearly done," but I fear and shudder because of the suffering yet to be endured by the people, and particularly women and children. There is no stopping of this war by the Southern people, and as long as a man can be raised to shoulder a gun it will be prosecuted and defended on the part of her people. If not on the present scale, it will be by falling back from State to State until the last man is subdued. You may rest assured of this,

The war became a prime focus of technology and production. Among the inventions developed during these years were the first railroad artillery, the first military telegraph, military railroads, the first land mines, telescopic sights for weapons,

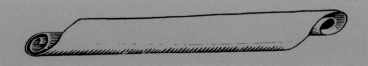

that unless the Yankee government desist from their purpose of subjugation, this war will never end. It is sad though, yet much more suffering than we have yet endured is to befall us all I am afraid. We are to realize the fact that we are engaged in war and that to yield will only make our condition far worse. I would much prefer now to see us thrown under the protection of the French government and as a consideration for her protection pay tribute of some kind. But I suppose our authorities know more that I on the subject and so long as my family are not in a starving condition I shall trust for this war to cease upon honorable terms and not other. No submission to tyrants has ever been our motto as Virginians. If the cause of the South is lost, all freedom of thought and speech is lost and we go back into the old monarchical forms of government. May the Almighty deliver us from our enemies and establish right and justice once more upon the earth, after passing through this terrible ordeal, is my only hope and prayer. He will stop this war in His own time and in His own way.

But I will close on this subject with the hope that you may all suffer as little as possible and that ere long the bright days of Peace may come and "we may be permitted to sit under our own vine and fig tree without any to make us afraid."

Source: "The Valley of the Shadow: The War Years," Augusta County, Virginia, Personal Papers, available online, www.valley.vcdh.virginia.edu.

The first major battle of the Civil War took place on July 21, 1861, at Bull Run, Virginia, when 35,000 Union troops marched southward into Virginia to capture Richmond, the capital of the Confederacy. The Confederate Army halted the Union advance and the battle ended in a Confederate victory.

and a new bullet—actually created in France—called the Minié bullet. This new bullet traveled farther and was more accurate than the musket balls and bayonets many soldiers used at the war's beginning.

The war may have provided a boom to factories, but it would prove devastating to those who owned the land through which the armies traveled. As supplies dwindled, hungry soldiers would seize whatever they could from the farms through which they passed, sometimes taking not only food, but also horses, clothing, and any weapons that could be found. A farmer might lose his entire livelihood if an army passed by near his home.

Lincoln had begun his presidency promising not to interfere with slavery in the South, but on September 22, 1862, he issued his Emancipation Proclamation announcing that, on January 1, 1863, "all persons held as slaves within any State, or designated part of a State, the people whereof shall then be in rebellion against the United States, shall be then, thenceforth, and forever free." Although the proclamation applied only to slaves in states that had seceded from the Union, it proved the first step in what would ultimately become the outlawing of slavery throughout the nation.

THE PRICE WE PAID

The Civil War deeply changed the United States, as Professor George Ticknor of Harvard noted in 1869. There was, he said, a "great gulf between what happened before in our century and what has happened since, or what is likely to happen hereafter. It does not seem to be as if I were living in the country in which I was born."[2] More than 3 million Americans fought in the Civil War, and 620,000 men died—2 percent of the population at the time. These almost unimaginable losses would devastate the United States for decades.

The Civil War was fought in some 10,000 different locations around the United States. North and South, East and West, all witnessed battles. Farms became battlefields, and homes became military headquarters. This war would leave scars on the countryside, and on the hearts and minds of the people who witnessed the fighting and the dying. The divisions between the two sides were not always neat or clear. The war divided not only states but also families: Sons might choose to fight on a different side from their father, or brother might face brother on opposing sides of a battle.

The war brought freedom to the slaves, but for many it was freedom in name only. Lacking skills, training, and education,

This artist's depiction shows Confederate soldiers rolling up their flag following General Lee's surrender at Appomattox in 1865.

many blacks found their lives little improved in the years immediately after the war. Constitutional amendments promised freedom and equality, but the reality was often segregation and poverty. Four million Americans were freed in the end, but it would be another 100 years before that freedom would begin to become a reality in the civil rights movement of the 1960s.

The war had brought an end to the economy that had shaped the South—a Southern plantation aristocracy. The United States that followed would be marked by a new focus on industrialization and the growth of both government and business. There was a post-war boom in the U.S. economy, a boom that benefited a select group of industrialists and made them very wealthy. Cities were flooded with people seeking work. Land was opened up for development in the West, but much of it fell into the hands of this wealthy few. Many opportunistic individuals hurried into the South as well, hoping to take advantage of its defeat, and those in the South suffered for many years in economic dependency and exploitation. During the war the South lost some $10 billion in property and nearly two-fifths of its livestock were destroyed.

Federal forces captured Jefferson Davis in Georgia in May 1865. He had been attempting to travel westward, where he thought he might be able to keep the war going. He was imprisoned for two years. When he was released, he spent time in Canada and England, and also traveled throughout the South. He served for a while as president of the Carolina Life Insurance Company. He was approached about serving as a senator from Mississippi and as president of what is now Texas A&M University, but declined both opportunities.

Davis wrote his memoirs, published as *The Rise and Fall of the Confederate Government*, and died on December 6, 1889, of pneumonia. Some 200,000 people attended his funeral in New Orleans. In 1893 his body was removed from its vault in the New Orleans cemetery and was taken to various state capitals, where it lay in state in Alabama, Georgia, and North Carolina. On May 31, 1893, the body finally reached Richmond, where Davis had served as president of the Confederacy. Davis's body was laid to rest after a procession witnessed by some 75,000 people. In 1978, Congress passed a joint resolution restoring Davis's U.S. citizenship.

Throughout the years that followed, Americans would disagree again and again over serious issues—sometimes bitterly. New states would again join the Union. The civil rights movement in the 1960s would spark new focus on the meaning of equality and the impact of race in America. But never again

This group of escaped slaves gathered on the former plantation of Confederate General Thomas Drayton. After federal troops occupied the plantation, these former slaves began to harvest and gin cotton for their own profit.

would one group of Americans face another on a U.S. battle-field. The Civil War had led, as Abraham Lincoln had hoped it would in his Gettysburg Address, to a "new birth of freedom."

CHRONOLOGY

1820   Missouri Compromise allows Missouri to be admitted as a slave state and Maine as a free state, while barring slavery from Northern territories.

1833   American Anti-Slavery Society is established.

1850   Compromise of 1850 admits California as a free state, establishes Utah and New Mexico as slave states, and requires return of fugitive slaves.

1854   Kansas-Nebraska Act repeals Missouri Compromise and allows popular vote to determine whether territories

TIMELINE

1820
Missouri admitted as a slave state and Maine as a free state.

1850
Compromise of 1850 admits California as a free state and establishes Utah and New Mexico without restrictions on slavery.

1820 — 1850

1833
American Anti-Slavery Society is established.

1854
Missouri Compromise is repealed. Popular vote will determine whether territories seeking statehood will be free or slave states.

seeking statehood will be free or slave states.

1857   *Dred Scott* decision by U.S. Supreme Court states that African Americans are not citizens and that Congress cannot ban slavery in any federal territories.

1859   John Brown leads unsuccessful raid on Harpers Ferry.

1860   South Carolina secedes from the Union after Abraham Lincoln is elected president.

1861   Confederate States of America is established, with Jefferson Davis as president. Civil War begins with the firing on U.S. troops at Fort Sumter.

1865   Civil War ends. Lincoln is assassinated.

1857
Dred Scott decided by U.S. Supreme Court.

1860
South Carolina secedes from the Union.

1865
Civil War ends. Lincoln is assassinated.

1860   1865

1859
John Brown leads unsuccessful raid on Harpers Ferry, Virginia.

1861
March 11
The Confederate States of America is established.

1861
April 12
The Civil War begins with the firing on U.S. troops at Fort Sumter.

NOTES

CHAPTER 1

1. Shelby Foote, *The Civil War: A Narrative* (New York: Random House, 1958), 6.
2. Ibid.
3. Letter from Jefferson Davis to Sarah Knox Taylor, Fort Gibson [Arkansas Territory], Dec. 16, 1834, part of *The Papers of Jefferson Davis*, available online at http://jeffersondavis.rice.edu.
4. Foote, *The Civil War*, 12.
5. Jefferson Davis's Remarks on Henry Clay's Resolutions, Senate Chamber, U.S. Capitol, January 29, 1850, from *The Papers of Jefferson Davis*, available online, http://jeffersondavis.rice.edu.
6. Foote, *The Civil War*, 16.
7. Jefferson Davis's Farewell Address, Senate Chamber, U.S. Capitol, January 21, 1861, from *The Papers of Jefferson Davis*, available online, http://jeffersondavis.rice.edu.
8. Foote, *The Civil War*, 17.

CHAPTER 2

1. David Brion Davis, *Inhuman Bondage: The Rise and Fall of Slavery in the New World* (New York: Oxford University Press, 2006), 124.
2. Ibid., 127.
3. Ibid., 129.
4. James Henry Hammond, "On the Admission of Kansas, Under the Lecompton Constitution ('Cotton is King')," speech before the United States Senate, March 4, 1858, available online, www.sewanee.edu/faculty/Willis/Civil_War/documents/HammdCotton.html.

CHAPTER 3

1. Geoffrey C. Ward, *The Civil War: An Illustrated History* (New York: Alfred A. Knopf, 1990), 12.
2. Scott Reynolds Nelson and Carol Sheriff, *A People at War: Civilians and Soldiers in America's Civil War, 1854–1877* (New York: Oxford University Press, 2007), 25.
3. Quoted in Ward, *The Civil War*, 19.
4. Nelson and Sheriff, *A People at War*, 5.
5. Quoted in Bruce Catton, *This Hallowed Ground* (New York: Doubleday, 1956), 2.
6. Ibid., 3.
7. Ibid.
8. Ibid., 6.
9. Ibid.

CHAPTER 4

1. Nelson and Sheriff, *A People at War*, 44.
2. Ward, 5.
3. Ibid.
4. Ibid., 6.
5. Quoted in "Dred Scott Case: The Supreme Court Decision," *Africans in America Resource Bank*, available online, www.pbs.org/wgbh/aia/part4.
6. Quoted in "Introduction to the Court Opinion on the Dred

Scott Case," available online,
http://usinfo.state.gov/usa/
infousa/facts/democrac/21.htm.
7. Nelson and Sheriff, *A People at War*, 41.

CHAPTER 5

1. Quoted in Joel H. Silbey, *A Respectable Minority: The Democratic Party in the Civil War Era, 1860–1868* (New York: W.W. Norton, 1977), 3.
2. Quoted in *Ibid.*, 4.
3. Quoted in Kenneth M. Stampp, ed., *The Causes of the Civil War* (Englewood Cliffs, NJ: Prentice-Hall, 1959), 29–30.
4. Quoted in Ibid., 181.

CHAPTER 6

1. Quoted in Horace Greeley, *The American Conflict: A History of the Great Rebellion in the United States of America, 1860–1864*, Vol. 1 (Hartford, CT: O.D. Case, 1864), 332.
2. Philip Van Doren Stern, ed., *The Life and Writings of Abraham Lincoln* (New York: Modern Library, 1940), 604.
3. Foote, *The Civil War*, 23.
4. Ibid.
5. Ibid., 27–28.
6. Quoted in Richard Carwardine, *Lincoln* (New York: Alfred A. Knopf, 2006), 80.
7. Quoted in *Ibid.*, 90.
8. David Herbert Donald and Harold Holzer, eds., *Lincoln in the Times: The Life of Abraham Lincoln as Originally Reported in The New York Times* (New York: St. Martin's Press, 2005), 47.
9. Ibid., 52.

10. Quoted in Bruce Catton, *The Coming Fury* (Garden City, NY: Doubleday, 1961), 222.

CHAPTER 7

1. Catton, *The Coming Fury*, 107.
2. Quoted in Stampp, *The Causes of the Civil War*, 37.
3. Quoted in Catton, *The Coming Fury*, 138.
4. Quoted in Ward, *The Civil War*, 27.
5. Ibid.
6. Quoted in Foote, *The Civil War*, 40–41.
7. Quoted in Ward, *The Civil War*, 30.
8. Ibid.

CHAPTER 8

1. Jefferson Davis, *The Rise and Fall of the Confederate Government*, Vol. 1, reprint edition (New York: Thomas Yoseloff, 1958).
2. Foote, *The Civil War*, 45.
3. Quoted in Ibid., 46.
4. Quoted in Ward, *The Civil War*, 36.
5. Quoted in Catton, *The Coming Fury*, 302.
6. Jefferson Davis, *The Rise and Fall of the Confederate Government*, 292.
7. Quoted in Ward, *The Civil War*, 38.
8. Quoted in Foote, *The Civil War*, 48.
9. Ibid.
10. Quoted in Ward, *The Civil War*, 39.

CHAPTER 9

1. Quoted in Ward, *The Civil War*, 383.
2. Ibid., 400.

BIBLIOGRAPHY

Baker, Jean H. *Affairs of Party: The Political Culture of Northern Democrats in the Mid-Nineteenth Century.* New York: Fordham University Press, 1998.

Baringer, William. *Lincoln's Rise to Power.* Boston: Little, Brown, 1937.

Basler, Roy P., ed. *The Collected Works of Abraham Lincoln.* Vol. 4. New Brunswick, N.J.: Rutgers University Press, 1953.

Carwardine, Richard. *Lincoln.* New York: Alfred A. Knopf, 2006.

Catton, Bruce. *The Civil War.* Boston: Houghton Mifflin, 1987.

———. *The Coming Fury.* Garden City, N.Y.: Doubleday, 1961.

———. *This Hallowed Ground.* New York: Doubleday, 1956.

Davis, David Brion. *Inhuman Bondage: The Rise and Fall of Slavery in the New World.* New York: Oxford University Press, 2006.

Davis, Jefferson. *The Rise and Fall of the Confederate Government.* Vol. 1. New York: Thomas Yoseloff, 1958 (reprint edition).

Davis, Michael. *The Image of Lincoln in the South.* Knoxville: University of Tennessee Press, 1971.

Donald, David Herbert. *Lincoln.* New York: Simon & Schuster, 1995.

Donald, David Herbert and Harold Holzer, eds. *Lincoln in the Times: The Life of Abraham Lincoln as Originally Reported in The New York Times.* New York: St. Martin's Press, 2005.

Foote, Shelby. *The Civil War: A Narrative.* New York: Random House, 1958.

Greeley, Horace. *The American Conflict: A History of the Great Rebellion in the United States of America, 1860–1864.* Vol. 1. Hartford, Conn.: O.D. Case, 1864.

Hansen, Harry. *The Civil War.* New York: New American Library, 1991.

Holzer, Harold, ed. *The Lincoln Mailbag: America Writes to the President, 1861–1865.* Carbondale: Southern Illinois University Press, 1998.

Library of Congress. "The African-American Mosaic Exhibition." Available online. URL: www.loc.gov/exhibits/african. Accessed May 16, 2008.

Marvel, William. *Mr. Lincoln Goes to War.* Boston: Houghton Mifflin, 2006.

McCarthy, Timothy Patrick and John Stauffer, eds. *Prophets of Protest: Reconsidering the History of American Abolitionism.* New York: The New Press, 2006.

The Museum of the Confederacy. Available online. URL: www.moc.org. Accessed May 16, 2008.

Mystic Seaport. "Exploring Amistad: Race and the Boundaries of Freedom in Antebellum Maritime America." Available online. URL: http://amistad.mysticseaport.org. Accessed May 16, 2008.

Nelson, Scott Reynolds and Carol Sheriff. *A People at War: Civilians and Soldiers in America's Civil War, 1854–1877.* New York: Oxford University Press, 2007.

Our Documents. Available online. URL: www.ourdocuments. gov. Accessed May 16, 2008.

PBS. "Africans in America." Available online. URL: www.pbs. org/wgbh/aia. Accessed May 16, 2008.

Scott, Col. Robert N., ed. *The War of the Rebellion: A Compilation of the Official Records of the Union and Confederate Armies.* Series 1. Vol. 1. Washington, D.C.: Government Printing Office, 1880.

Silbey, Joel H. *A Respectable Minority: The Democratic Party in the Civil War Era, 1860–1868.* New York: W.W. Norton, 1977.

Sojourner Truth Institute. Available online. URL: www. sojournertruth.org. Accessed May 16, 2008.

Stampp, Kenneth M., ed. *The Causes of the Civil War.* Englewood Cliffs, N.J.: Prentice-Hall, 1959.

Stern, Philip Van Doren, ed. *The Life and Writings of Abraham Lincoln.* New York: Modern Library, 1940.

University of Virginia, Institute for Advanced Technology in the Humanities. Available online. URL: www.iath.virginia. edu. Accessed May 16, 2008.

Ward, Geoffrey C. *The Civil War.* New York: Alfred A. Knopf, 1990.

FURTHER READING

Catton, Bruce. *Bruce Catton's Civil War.* New York: Phoenix Press, 2001.

Davis, William C. (ed.). *Shadows of the Storm.* Garden City, N.Y.: Doubleday, 1981.

Foote, Shelby. *The Civil War: A Narrative.* New York: Vintage Books, 1986.

Hyslop, Steve. *Eyewitness to the Civil War.* Washington, D.C.: National Geographic, 2006.

Ward, Geoffrey C. *The Civil War.* New York: Alfred A. Knopf, 1990.

WEB SITES

Abraham Lincoln Historical Digitization Project
http://lincoln.lib.niu.edu

The African-American Mosaic Exhibition
http://www.loc.gov/exhibits/african

Civil War Women: Primary Sources on the Internet
http://library.duke.edu/specialcollections/bingham/guides/cwdocs.html

Crisis at Fort Sumter
http://www.tulane.edu/~sumter

Documenting the American South
http://docsouth.unc.edu

The Museum of the Confederacy
http://www.moc.org

PBS: Africans in America
http://www.pbs.org/wgbh/aia

INDEX

abolition movement, 16–22
American Anti-Slavery Society, 19–20
Anderson, Robert, 73–74, 75–77, 80–82, 83–84
Appeal to the Coloured Citizens of the World (Walker), 21–22
Appomattox Court House, 83

Beauregard, P.G.T., 80–82
Benjamin, Judah P., 69
Black Hawk (Chief), 5
Bleeding Kansas, 28–34
Booth, John Wilkes, 84
Boyce, William, 53
Breckinridge, John, 47, 56
Brierfield, 1, 5, 8
Brooks, Preston, 34
Brown, John, 35–38
Buchanan, James, 43, 58, 72–74, 78–79
Bull Run, Battle of, 84–86
bullets, 88
Butler, Andrew, 31–34

Calhoun, John C., 27
California, 27
Campbell, John, 75–76
Carolina Life Insurance Company, 91
Clay, Henry, 7–8
Cobb, Howell, 68
Compromise of 1850, 26–28
Confederate States of America, 10–11, 67–71
cotton gin, 19

"Cotton is King" speech, 16–17, 19
Crawford, Martin J., 72
"Crime Against Kansas" speech, 32–33

Davis, Jefferson
    death of, 91
    early life of, 1–4
    military career of, 4–6
    military forts and, 72–73, 76–80
    as president of Confederate States of America, 10–11, 67–71
    secession and, 8–10
    as senator, 6–8
Davis, Samuel E., 2
Davis, Varina, 1, 6, 11
Declaration of Independence, slavery and, 15
"Declaration of the Causes of Secession," 70–71
Democratic Party, 44–45, 49, 56
Douglas, Stephen, 28–29, 43, 47, 55–56
Douglass, Frederick, 22, 35–36
Dred Scott v. Sandford, 38–39, 50, 56
Dutch
    slavery and, 12–13, 20

economy
    results of Civil War and, 90–91
    slavery and, 13, 16–17, 19, 23–24

About the Author

HEATHER LEHR WAGNER is a writer and an editor. She earned a master's degree in government from the College of William and Mary and a bachelor's degree in political science from Duke University. She is the author of more than 40 books exploring political and social issues.

Photo Credits